Imperial Glass Lace Edge

Laura J. Marsh

4880 Lower Valley Road, Atglen, PA 19310 USA

Dedication

To my Mother and Father who, side by side, used their beautiful Crocheted Crystal to serve family and friends on numerous wonderful occasions.

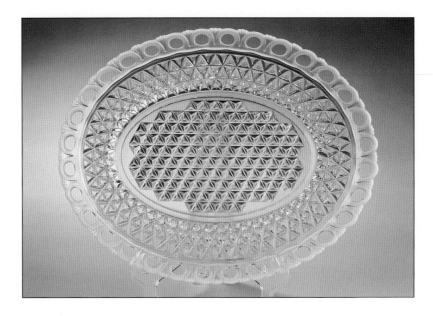

Published by Schiffer Publishing Ltd.
4880 Lower Valley Road
Atglen, PA 19310
Phone: (610) 593-1777; Fax: (610) 593-2002
E-mail: Info@schifferbooks.com

For the largest selection of fine reference books on this and related subjects, please visit our web site at
www.schifferbooks.com
We are always looking for people to write books on new and related subjects. If you have an idea for a book please contact us at the above address.

This book may be purchased from the publisher.
Include $3.95 for shipping.
Please try your bookstore first.
You may write for a free catalog.

In Europe, Schiffer books are distributed by
Bushwood Books
6 Marksbury Ave.
Kew Gardens
Surrey TW9 4JF England
Phone: 44 (0) 20 8392-8585; Fax: 44 (0) 20 8392-9876
E-mail: info@bushwoodbooks.co.uk
Free postage in the U.K., Europe; air mail at cost.

Designed by Mark David Bowyer
Type set in University Roman Bd BT/Humanist521 BT

ISBN: 0-7643-2027-0
Printed in China
1 2 3 4

Contents

Acknowledgments

To my husband Terry, for sharing the fun of the hunt for glass and for knowing it was time for me to write a book.

To Eric, Kristin, Brittany, and Kyle and to Andrew, Lara, and Alexandra, our family, for their encouragement, and especially to Kristin for reading the manuscript so carefully.

To my sister Dorothy Williams, for buying me that first piece of purple slag Lace Edge.

To my sister Roberta Oliven, for her continuing enthusiasm and support.

To Joan Cimini, for answering endless questions, sending me information, reading the manuscript, and giving valuable comments.

To Myrna and Bob Garrison, for offering information and sympathizing with the process of preparing a volume for print.

To Marlene DeFrenn, for urging me to write this book and finding pieces of Lace Edge.

To Jackie and Tom Norland, Bunny Wustefeld, Monte and Kris Schroer, and all the Fox Valley Study Group members, for helping me discover more about Lace Edge.

To Ed and Audrey Lautenschlager, for solving an identification puzzle that had all of us stumped.

To Wandeen and Gene Davis, for sharing their love of Lace Edge.

To Mary Lee Wilson, for her eagerness and interest in what I was researching.

To the West Virginia Museum of American Glass and Dean Six, for making Imperial catalogs readily available for research.

To the Rakow Library and Beth Hylen, for helping me on my adventure of two years of Interlibrary Loans so that I could review all that fiche.

To the North Central College Library and June Johnson, for facilitating the Interlibrary Loans.

To the Chicago Historical Society, for access to their collection of Sears catalogs.

To Dan Stultz of Stultz Photography, for his good nature during long hours of taking pictures.

To Stan, my horse, for being my escape from thinking about glass.

Preface

My father worked for Sears, Roebuck and Company for thirty-seven years, so it should have come as no surprise when I discovered some years later that my mother's beautiful pieces of crystal were purchased from Sears. When I inherited those pieces of Crocheted Crystal, I had no idea of the odyssey on which they would lead me. First of all, there was the surprising discovery that glass that looked like Crocheted Crystal was also made in color. My sister presented me with a purple slag bowl that she had found in an antique store. The loops and paneling looked the same as our mother's familiar pieces.

When I started looking, pale colors, deep colors, and also caramel slag appeared in pieces similar to what I had, as well as many other shapes. Then there were all those looped-edge pieces that did not have paneled sides. Little diamonds, big triangles, and hexagon-shaped dots covered pieces with those same loops. Some pieces had completely plain sides and those same loops around the edge. As I tried to find information about this variety of pieces, my reading led me to the Imperial Glass Corporation and their line called Lace Edge. Then I came upon the website for the National Imperial Glass Collectors Society, Inc. (NIGCS). This led to my attending the annual convention and then finding a local NIGCS study group.

Not knowing what names to use for the shapes or patterns, I tried to figure out a way to categorize my pieces. In frustration, I set five pieces side-by-side. The pieces were similar in size, and each had four toes, panels, and loops. The sides of one piece were simply flared out, while another was pinched together under the loops. The flare of another piece was crimped into six sections, so the edge waved up and down. Another was shaped into a square at the top, and the loops on the last piece were turned toward the inside. I posed the question at the next meeting of the NIGCS study group. Could all five pieces have come from the same mould? Certainly possible, came the answer. How can I find out the mould number? No source was obvious.

Thus began my research into Imperial's catalogs. Joan Cimini, Director of the National Imperial Glass Museum, shared copies of her personal collection of catalogs. Through Interlibrary Loan I reviewed the Rakow Library's collections of catalogs transferred to microfiche when the Imperial factory was closing. The West Virginia Museum of American Glass was another source of catalogs. Over time, categories began to emerge. For example, although most catalogs did not mention colors, it became possible to predict the range of colors for specific shapes and sizes, based on the mould numbers. The proof came in determining the mould numbers for the pieces in my growing collection and seeing that the colors were as predicted.

The following pages display the results of my research. The collector can find the information needed to identify the pieces in her collection and understand what she is likely to find on her next shopping trip. Because Imperial made some glass which was never shown in a catalog or price list, and, unfortunately, catalogs, price lists, and records of manufacture have been lost over time, there is no way to be certain that every mould number for Lace Edge is found on these pages. There is always more to learn.

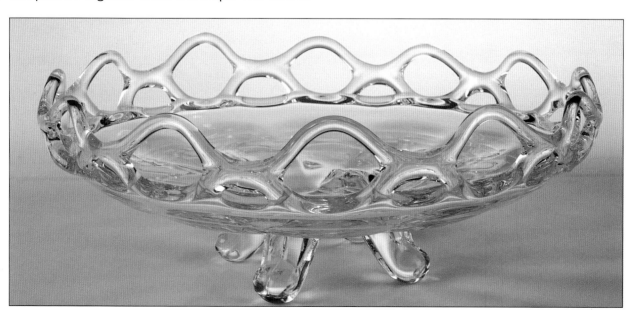

Chapter 1

History of Lace Edge

The Imperial Glass Company produced Lace Edge pieces over a period of more than forty years, from the early 1930s to the late 1970s. Imperial used the name Lace Edge for a variety of different pieces, all of which had an open, lacey edge. After the first twenty years, the name was used less frequently, for the pieces were often identified only by color, not pattern name. This book will cover all Imperial Lace Edge and related pieces.

Lace Edge began production near the end of the Depression. Starting a new line in hard times was a bold move that turned out to be very successful. Lace Edge continued to play an active role in Imperial's selection of glass produced for many years.

Names Used Over Time by Imperial and Per Other Authors

The earliest extant catalog pages including Lace Edge pieces date from the late 1930s. Several pages depict pieces with mould numbers beginning with 743, 745, 749, or 780 and label them "Hand Made Laced Edge Pattern" or "Imperial Laced Edge Pattern." Because Imperial made three of the 745 pieces with a special design in honor of the 1934 Bellaire Centennial Celebration, it is clear that Lace Edge was in production by at least 1934.

Another late-1930s catalog page calls some of the 743 and 745 pieces "New Imperial Novelties," with the sub-title "Four-Toed Laced Edged Vases" for the 743 vases. The Milk Glass 745s earn the name "Real Useful Novelties." If the collector sees 745 pieces for sale as Novelties, the reason may lie in the old catalogs.

The Milk Glass 743s did not come under the heading of Laced Edge in these catalog pages. Imperial was consistent in using only the label Milk Glass for most open edge pieces when Milk Glass came back into production in the 1950s. There were occasional exceptions to this practice. Later, for a 1965 Milk Glass special sale, the items are called "Ten of Imperial's Most Wanted Open-Edged Pieces."

To fill up a catalog page and add variety, Imperial sometimes pictured pieces unrelated to the main group or title of the page. Such was the case with the "Hand Made Laced Edge Pattern" page. This grouping included a 761 Compote, which did not have an open edge. The "New Imperial Novelties" page shows a 145 Chicken-on-Nest, again with no open edge. Another page of 749s includes the unre-lated 779 3-Toed Ash Receiver and a 1664 1/2 3-piece Mayonnaise Set.

Only the "New Imperial Novelties" page referred to colors besides Crystal. These 743 and 745 pieces were available in six colors. The collector can find these and many other Lace Edge pieces in colors not listed in catalogs or price lists. This creates a challenge for the collector, who can never be quite sure what she will find for sale.

The 749 pieces with the crow's foot edge currently command the highest prices of any Lace Edge pieces, but in 1936 they were given away for coupons found in Friedman's Oak Grove or Cream of Nut margarine, according to the *Imperial Glass Encyclopedia* discussion of Lace Edge. Some of the 749 pieces with the crossed loops were included in the offer. One color was available, Seafoam Blue. Seafoam Green crow's foot pieces are even more rare and expensive, perhaps because they were not so widely distributed.

The 1957 Supplement Page E, dated January 1, 1957, advertised the Collectors Cupboard items. One of these was the 749C 7" Lace Edge Comporte, but it was the only Lace Edge item in the group. A related piece, 785 Covered Candy Box, Open Edge, was also part of the special listing. See Chapter 7 Related Pieces by Imperial for more information about that piece. The Collectors Cupboard items were available in four colors: Midwest Rose, Honey Amber, Wistar Purple, and Steigel Green.

In 1968 another special group was presented, and all the pieces were identified as Lace Edge. Imperial salesmen used this picture to promote sales. A company memo to the salesmen stated that these Belmont Crystal items were not to be offered to regular retailers. With their bargain prices, these items were more suitable for discounters and what the June 1968 Price List calls "Mass Merchandisers." Some of the pieces were from the standard Lace Edge line, but six were produced just for this promotion. The colors were not standard colors, however. The Price List says that Belmont Crystal was available in Honey and Olive. Refer to Chapter 5 Mould Number List and Pictures for the complete range of colors for pieces from the standard line.

As noted, all the early pages used "Laced Edge" and not "Lace Edge." The "d" was dropped from Imperial publications during the 1940s. Since the National Imperial Glass Collectors Society, Inc. (NIGCS) refers to the name as Lace Edge in their *Imperial Glass Encyclopedia,* this book will follow that custom.

BELMONT CRYSTAL

Top Row: 7499D 14" Plate, 7497D 11" Plate, 7436D 9" Plate
Second Row: 7436F 7 1/2" Bowl, 7497F 9" Bowl, 7499F 11 1/2" Bowl, 7490 2-Lite Candleholder
Third Row: 7430B 5" 4-Toed Vase, 7435C 6 1/2" 4-Toed Compote, 7435 4-Toed Candy Box & Cover
Bottom Row: 7497/9 2-Tier Tid Bit (14" and 11" Plates), 7436K 6" Flower Arranger (with frog), 7436
7" Candy Box & Cover, 7436C 7 1/2" Bowl (*Names of pieces are Belmont names*)

Imperial used the Lace Edge pattern name to refer to various open-edged pieces. Included in Chapter 5 Mould Number List and Pictures are the 743, 745, 749, and 780 series and their variations. Look to Chapter 7 Related Pieces by Imperial for other pieces that may resemble Lace Edge as well as dissimilar pieces called Lace Edge. Found in that chapter also is a list of Imperial documents researched and what name was used for Lace Edge pieces in each.

The confusion over how to refer to Lace Edge items is widespread among collectors. Using the term "Novelties" for some pieces has already been mentioned. However, its use has by no means been restricted to the items that appeared on the catalog pages under that heading. Hazel Marie Weatherman coined the term "Sugar Cane" to refer to the 745 pieces and "Katy" to refer to some of the 749 pieces in her *Colored Glassware of the Depression Era, Book 2,* but over the years collectors have freely extended the application of those terms. Sometimes people use the name Katy for all Lace Edge or all 749s. Other times, Katy covers all Seafoam Blue or Seafoam Green pieces, whatever the number. Rather than try to redefine any of these terms, I choose to omit them and simply use "Lace Edge" with Imperial's numbers.

Patents

The United States Patent Office records show the existence of at least three patents awarded to Imperial Glass Corporation for Lace Edge pieces. A patent was usually applied for after a piece was successfully in production. Mould numbers were not included in patent documentation.

Under the category Design for a Bowl or Similar Article is a patent granted June 25, 1935, after the application dated April 12, 1935. This patent, 96,048, is for the 749 Sugar. Under the category Design for a Plate or Similar Article is a patent granted July 2, 1935, after the application dated March 29, 1935. This patent, 96,132, is for the 7496D 8" Salad Plate. Both these designs had the crow's foot lace edge and triangles on the sides. The terms of the patents were for seven years, but these pieces were not seen in Imperial catalogs after 1940 and are prized by collectors.

An application was also filed May 28, 1942, under the category Design for a Hurricane Lamp Adapter for Candlesticks or Similar Article. This application resulted in a patent being granted on September 29, 1942. Number 133,956 was issued for a term of fourteen years. The item does not appear in any existing Imperial catalogs, price lists, or salesman's notebooks, but the National Imperial Glass Museum in Bellaire, Ohio, has this adapter. It does not stand alone but has a narrow base to fit into a candle holder. The top of the adapter looks like a 7802 candleholder and has a deep ridge to hold a hurricane lamp securely in place around the candle.

A note dated 1944 on a page from Imperial photo notebooks refers to the open-handled 780 Punch Cup and states that "This punch cup was once patented." My research has yet to find this patent number and date.

Chapter 2

Sears and Other Vendors

According to records of old orders, Sears, Roebuck and Company carried Lace Edge as early as 1939. The 7498F 3-piece Console Set was part of an order dated March 16, 1939. Sears assigned its own number (R790) instead of the Imperial mould number.

Imperial produced a pattern for Sears that first appeared in their Fall and Winter catalog for 1943-1944. Imperial used their own 780 mould numbers for these pieces but also used the 1700 numbers assigned by Sears for their catalogs. Order forms show listings by both sets of numbers. Neither the name Lace Edge nor the name of the manufacturer was mentioned in the catalogs or in Sears stores.

Sears called the pattern Crocheted and later Crocheted Crystal. Pieces carried a special label which was attached at the Imperial factory and read, "Crocheted Hand Made Crystal" along with the words "Harmony House," a Sears brand. An undated Sears advertisement explained, "This pattern has been named 'Crocheted' – our own name for the elegantly famous old design now reproduced exclusively for Sears in new beauty, brilliance, and variety. Each piece carries this label stating that it is hand-made."

This ad was found in a notebook of photographs collected for Imperial. A note is typed onto the ad that says "Stemware by Central." Imperial bought stemware moulds from Central Glass Works in 1940. It is reasonable to conclude that the Crocheted Crystal stemware came from former Central moulds, modified for this purpose. Look at Chapter 5 Mould Number List and Pictures to see how the Crocheted Crystal pattern is obvious in the stemware.

Many of the Crocheted Crystal pieces sold in Sears stores were parts of sets sold in the catalogs. Buyers in the stores could buy the three pieces to have their own mayonnaise sets or just buy a replacement bowl, plate, or ladle. Other pieces sold in the stores were not available in the catalogs but did carry the special Crocheted Crystal labels.

The last Sears catalog to list Crocheted Crystal was Spring and Summer of 1950. Although the earliest listing had shown thirty-two items, the last showed only five. The scarcity or abundance of all these pieces relates to how long they were sold.

Here is the list of the items sold through the catalogs, with the dual numbers and names. Catalog dates are indicated by these letters:

"A" means the item appeared only in the Fall and Winter 1943-44.

"B" means the item appeared through Spring and Summer 1949, except for Christmas 1948.

"C" means the item appeared through Spring and Summer 1950, except for Fall and Winter 1948-49 and Christmas 1948.

"D" means the item appeared in every catalog.

"E" means the item appeared through the date shown, whether a Fall and Winter (F/W) or Spring and Summer (S/S) catalog.

"F" means the pieces had old and new versions. Catalog dates for items marked with an F are shown after the list.

Mould #	Item in Imperial Cat.	Sears #	Item in Sears Cat.	Date
780	12 oz. Ftd. Ice Tea	1750	Footed Ice Tea	C
780	5 1/2 oz. Tall Sherbet	1750	Sherbet	C
780	4 1/2 oz. Claret Wine	1750	Wine	C
780	3 1/2 oz. Cocktail	1750	Cocktail	A
780	5 1/2 oz. Ftd. Juice Tumbler	1750	Fruit Juice	A
780	10 oz. Goblet	1750	Goblet	C
780	Sugar and Creamer Set old style	1726	Sugar & Creamer Set	A
780	Sugar and Creamer Set new style	1752	Sugar &Creamer Set	F
780	Punch Cup-old style	1720	Cup	F
780	Punch Cup-new style	1720	Cup	F
780C	2-pc. Epergne	1727	Epergne	B
780D	12 1/2" Ftd. Cake Stand	1729	Cake Stand	D
7800	11 1/2" Relish Dish	1715	Oblong Relish Dish	A
7800	3-pc Mayonnaise Set 7 1/2" Plate, 5" Bowl, Ladle	1705	Mayonnaise Set	D
7800	Starter Set 4 ea. Goblet, Sherbet, 8" Plate	1751	Starter Set	C
7801	10 /2" Hors d'oeuvres round	1716	Hors d'oeuvres Dish	B
7802	10" Celery Dish	1717	Celery Dish	A
7802/0	7 3/4" Basket	1725	Fruit/Flower Basket	A
7805D	8" Plate	1700	Salad Plate	C
7806/0	9 1/2" Basket	1724	Fruit/Flower Basket	A
7806D	9 1/2" Plate	1701	Plate	B
7808/0	12 1/2" or 13" Basket	1723	Fruit/Flower Basket	A
7808/9	4-pc Salad Set 10 1/2" Bowl, 13/12" Plate, Fork, Spoon	1732	4-pc Salad Set	B

Mould #	Item in Imperial Cat.	Sears #	Item in Sears Cat.	Date
7808B	8" Trumpet Bouquet	1731	Vase-Trumpet Shape	A
7808F	3-pc Console 11" Shallow Bowl, Twin Candleholders	1739	3 pc Console Set	D
7808K	7" Narcissus Bowl	1714	Narcissus Bowl	E F/W 47-48
7809	3-pc Buffet Set 14" Plate, Compote, Ladle	1736	3-pc Buffet Set	B
7809	2-pc Cheese and Cracker 12" Plate, Ftd. Compote	1735	Cheese and Cracker Set	A
7809C	12" Crimped Bowl	1737	Bowl-Wavy Edge	E S/S 44
7809D	14" Plate	1703	Plate	E S/S 49
78010	14-piece Punch Set	1719	14-pc Punch Set	F
78010D	17" Plate	1704	Plate	E S/S 49
7802	Candleholder Crimped and lamp	1718	Hurricane Lamps	A
n/a	3-pc Console Set	1738	3-pc Console Set Hurricane Lamps & Bowl	A

The Punch Set is marked with an F because the set with the older style of cup appeared until Spring and Summer 1946 but with the newer style of cup from Fall and Winter 1946-1947 until the last catalog in Spring and Summer 1950. The newer cup by itself was sold in those same catalogs. The newer style of Sugar and Creamer is marked F and was sold in only two catalogs, Spring and Summer 1948 and Fall and Winter 1948-1949.

Second, here is the list of the items sold in Sears stores, with the dual numbers and names.

Mould #	Item in Imperial Catalog	Sears #	Item in Sears Store
615	5" Ladle	1705	Mayonnaise Ladle
701	Fork and Spoon	1733	Fork and Spoon
703	Punch Ladle	1721	Punch Ladle
780	5" Bowl - Mayonnaise Set	1705	Mayonnaise Bowl
780	4 1/2" Candleholder (Twin)	1708	Candleholder
780	Oyster Cocktail	1750	Oyster Cocktail
780	Epergne Vase	1727	Epergne Vase
780C	Epergne Bowl	1727	Epergne Bowl
780C	Hurricane Lamps	1718	Lamps
780F	10" Footed Fruit Stand	1728	Footed Fruit Stand
7801W	7 1/2" Comport, 4-Toed	1713	Comport, 4-Toed
7802C	Saucer Candle (Crimped)	1707	Saucer Candle
7802D	7 1/2" Plate	1705	Mayonnaise Plate
7802F	6 1/2" Nappy (Shallow)	1710	Nappy
7803B	5" Vase, 4-Toed, Belled Top (Violet Bowl)	1712	Vase, 4-Toed
7804B	6 1/2" Ftd. Jelly	1711	Ftd. Jelly

Mould #	Item in Imperial Catalog	Sears #	Item in Sears Store
7806F	8" Walnut Bowl	1709	Walnut Bowl
7808C	3-pc Console -10" Crimped Bowl, Twin Candleholders	1739	3-pc Console
7000D	13" Plate (was 12")	1702	13" Plate
7808F	11" Bowl, Shallow, Plain Bottom	1706	Bowl, Shallow, Plain Bottom
7808K	8" Bud Bouquet	1730	Bud Bouquet
7809B	10 1/2" Salad Bowl	1734	Salad Bowl
78010B	Punch Bowl	1722	Punch Bowl

It should be noted that Sears did not carry any of the 780 pieces with intaglio, cuts, metal attachments, decals, flashing, or colors. There were also some plain crystal 780 pieces that were not in the Sears Crocheted Crystal line but were sold elsewhere.

While other vendors were not allowed to use the name Crocheted Crystal, order forms from the 1940s show that Sears was not the only vendor to buy certain 780 pieces. For example, retailer Montgomery Ward and Company and distributor Butler Brothers ordered the 780 Twin Candleholders and the 7800 3-piece Mayonnaise Set. Eight companies bought the 7801W 7 1/2" Compote and the 7806D 9 1/2" Plate in Crystal or other colors.

Records also show three companies besides Sears ordered the 7802F 6 1/2" Nappy (Shallow). Silvalyte coated that bowl and several other shapes with their own type of finish. The Marion Glass Manufacturing Company, which cut and sandblasted designs on glassware, and Butler Brothers were the others buyers. See Chapter 6 Additions to Lace Edge Pieces for more information on further processing after the glass left the Imperial factory.

Imperial records from around 1940 list dozens of department and variety stores, wholesalers, lighting manufacturers, metal companies, and other customers buying 743, 745, 749, and 780 Lace Edge from Imperial. Like Sears, Butler Brothers had enough status as a buyer to have their own numbering system used on Imperial order forms. Order Number 50X-4517, for example, was called a Hand Cut Crystal Assortment. This order contained these items, along with two other pieces that were not Lace Edge:

Mould #	Item
7802D/cut 272	7 1/2" Plate
7802F/cut 272	6 1/2" Nappy
7802B/cut 272	6 1/2" Bowl
7803B/cut 272	5" Vase

Butler Brothers ordered at least one item not produced for other buyers. According to a copy of a Butler Brothers May-June 1936 catalog reproduced in Naomi L. Over's *Ruby Glass of the 20th Century*, they offered a piece that would have been designated as a 745E. It was called a Basket Shape Bon Bon Dish, 7 in., and is not documented in extant Imperial catalogs or order forms.

The catalog group was number 50R-4515. All pieces in the group were Ruby. Other Lace Edge items pictured were 7455D 7 1/2" Plate, which they called a Mini Bowl, 7 in. – Lace Edge, and the 7455F 6 3/4" Nappy, which they dubbed the Round Nappy, 6 1/2 in. – Lace Edge. The group included other pieces that were not Lace Edge.

According to a salesman's notebook list of what Butler Brothers ordered in 1939, they were still buying this group by number from Imperial. The number does not appear on the 1940 list. Ruby is the only color known for the special 745E basket bowl. Like the other Imperial pieces sold by Butler Brothers, this dish was credited to Imperial in their catalog.

Besides the many vendors of Imperial's Lace Edge in the United States, stores outside the country carried it as well. No documentation backs up the suggestion that Lace Edge was sold in England, but orders from around 1940 exist for shipment to Cuba and Canada. The list below shows an order for the 780 Line shipped to Canada. Note that numbers and names are not always consistent.

Mould #	Item
7804B	6 1/2" Ftd. Jelly
7802F	6 1/2" Bon Bon
780	Sugar and Cream (old style)
7801W	4-toed Compote
7808F	11" Bowl
7808D	12" Plate
7809D	14" Plate
7803B	5" Violet Bowl
7809	2-pc. Cheese & Cracker
7808B	8" Vase
7801	10 1/2" Relish
7806D	9 1/2" Plate
7800	3-pc. Mayonnaise Set
7809	3-pc. Buffet Set
701	Fork & Spoon
7806F	8" Bowl
780	10" Celery Tray
780	4 1/2" Twin Candle
780	11 1/2" Oblong Relish
7802D	7 1/2" Plate
7808/9	2-pc. Bowl & Plate Set
7802C	2-pc. Hurricane Lamps
78010	15-pc. Punch Set

Chapter 3

Understanding Mould Numbers

Describing an average piece of Imperial's Lace Edge to a potential collector is not an easy task, for there is no standard item. No common mould number, pattern, edge, or shape applies to all Lace Edge. Imperial used the name for a variety of pieces over many years and sometimes produced identical pieces but did not call them Lace Edge. Certain criteria can illustrate the pieces produced, in terms of mould number prefixes, base measurements, letters for edgings, intaglio numbers, and cut numbers.

Pattern Types

745 745: Ivy Ball, Stiegel Green, $14-16

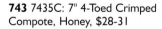

743 7435C: 7" 4-Toed Crimped Compote, Honey, $28-31

This table shows the Lace Edge mould numbers. Note that 780 is meant to include the 78 numbers also. For each prefix, a standard pattern was used for the sides of the pieces and a standard lace edging employed. Production of Lace Edge continued for four decades, and some early mould numbers were replaced with other numbers when similar pieces were made later in new colors. Refer to Chapter 5 Mould Number List and Pictures for examples of all these pattern types.

7494, 7495, 7496, 74910 7496W: 7" Soup Bowl, Flared, Seafoam Blue, $40-45

Mould #	Sides	Lace Edging
743	diamonds	curves crossing
745	hexagons & squares	curves crossing
7494, 7495, 7496, 74910	triangles	crow's foot
7497, 7498, 7499	triangles	curves crossing
780 (except 7805 with no panels)	optic panels	curves crossing
7805, except 7805D	no panels	curves crossing

7497, 7498, 7499 7497B: 9" Bowl, Ruby, $32-35

780 (except 7805 items with no paneling)
780: 6" Covered Bowl, Rubigold Carnival, $40-45

7805 items with no paneling 7805W: 5 1/2" Deep Bowl, Ritz Blue, $18-21

Base Measurements

The base of this 7802B Bowl measures 3".

Because all the pieces that share a mould number come from identical moulds, it stands to reason that the measurements across their bases would be the same. Knowing the distance across the base can help to confirm proper identification of each piece. For some mould prefixes, all pieces had the same base size. For other prefixes, the additional digits of the number are required to match the base measurement. This list shows the prefixes or numbers and the base sizes. The 7805* refers to pieces with no paneling.

Mould #	Base Size
743	3 3/4"
745	3"
7494	2 1/2"
7495	4"
7496	4 3/4"
7497	4 1/4"
7498	5 1/4"
74910	5 3/4"
7802	3"
7805	3 3/4"
7805*	3"
7806	3 3/4"
7808	5 1/4"
7809	4 1/4"
78010	5"

Letters

B 7803B: 5" Vase, 4-Toed, Belled Top, Crystal, $22-25

Imperial used letters after the mould numbers to indicate the kinds of pieces made. Moulds usually formed belled bowls. The glass workers shaped the pliable results into a variety of shapes before the further processing. This table lists the letters used for Lace Edge and defines the shapes of the corresponding pieces.

Letter	Description
B	Belled bowl or vase
C	Crimped
D	Flat plate or cake stand
E	Basket bowl or banana bowl – 2 sides up, 2 out
F	Shallow bowl with upright lace edge
G	Belled bowl with upright lace edge
K	Flower bowl or vase, pinched below lace edge
N	Flower bowl or vase, lace edge turned in
R	Flower bowl or vase, lace edge curved down and out
S	Squared bowl
V	Plate with turned up lace edge
W	Same as B
X	Flanged edge, or lace straight out
Z	Same as N

C 7801C: 7 1/2" Compote, 4-Toed, Crimped, Crystal, $28-31

D 7802D: 7 1/2" Plate, Crystal, $14-16

E 7497E: 9 1/2" Basket Bowl, Crystal, $28-31

F 7455F: 6 3/4" Nappy, Crystal, $18-20

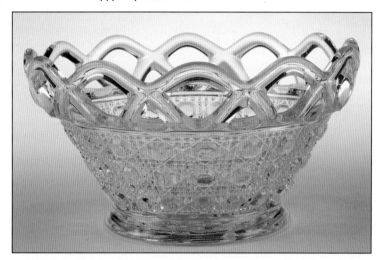

G 7455G: 6" Basket Bowl, Crystal, $18-20

K 7497K: 6 1/2" Rose Bowl, Crystal, $28-31

N 743N: 5 1/2" Vase, 4-Toed, Crystal, $28-31

R 7497R: 6 1/2" Flower Bowl, Crystal, $28-31

S 7801S: 6" Square Bon Bon,
4-Toed, Crystal, $28-31

V 7498/97V: Tid Bit Set found with two upper plates
instead of one larger and one smaller, Crystal, $70-75

W 7495W: 5 1/2" Cereal
Bowl, Crystal, $2-4

X 743X: 4 1/2" Vase, 4-Toed, Crystal, $28-31

Z 7801Z: 4 1/2" Rose Bowl, 4-Toed, Crystal, $28-31

Intaglio Numbers

The base of the mould pressed a pattern of leaves with fruit or flowers into the base of some pieces of glass. The pattern was then washed with acid to etch the design and make it more obvious. If a piece had an intaglio base, Imperial assigned a number designating the intaglio pattern. The intaglio number was added to the end of the mould numbers and preceded by a slash. The letter indicating the type of piece followed the intaglio number. Each intaglio pattern was used only with certain mould numbers. Refer to Chapter 5 Mould Number List and Pictures to learn more. Note that intaglio is almost always found only on Crystal pieces.

This list indicates the four known intaglio numbers and the matching patterns. The Bellaire Centennial design in the base of three Crystal 745 pieces is not etched with acid and so is not included in this list as intaglio. The illustration shows the difference.

4 7498/4F: 11" Bowl, Shallow, Crystal, $21-23

#/#	Intaglio
#/3	Apple and Pear
#/4	Grapes
#/5	Roses
#/6	Vegetables

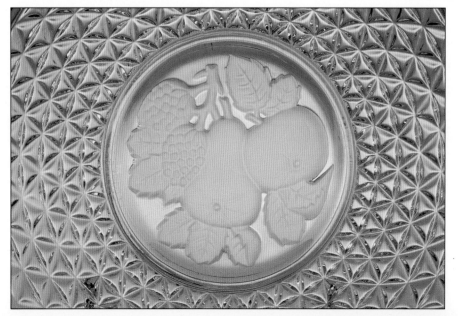

3 7497/3D: 11" Plate, Crystal, $21-23

5 7436/5D: 9 1/2" Plate, Crystal, $21-23

6 780/6: 11 1/2" Relish, Crystal, $25-28

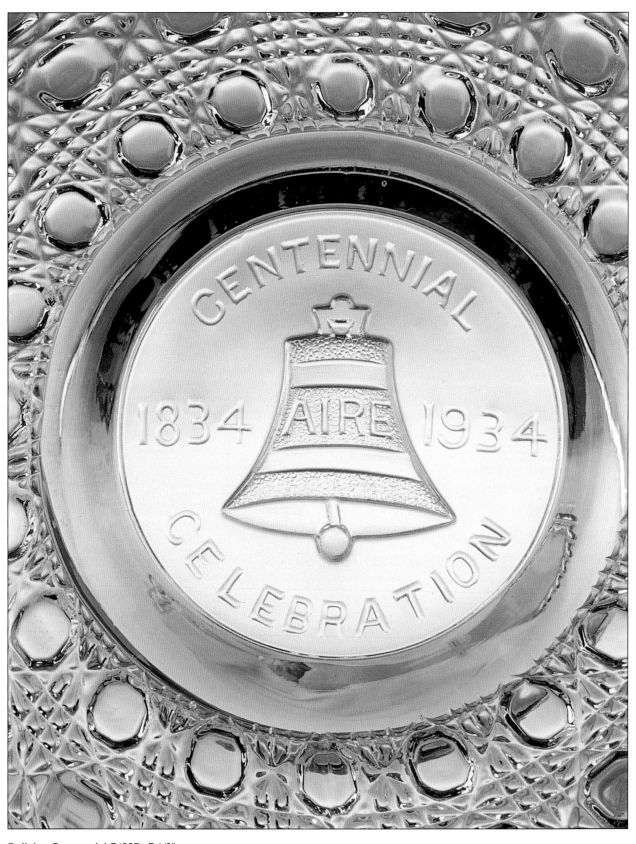

Bellaire Centennial 7455D: 7 1/2"
Plate, Crystal, $18-21

Cut Numbers

All Lace Edge pieces with cuts are Crystal 780 pieces. A suffix with an identifying number (e.g., /cut 120) was added to the mould number for each cut piece. Catalog 1936(?)-40(?) shows many of the cuts done by Imperial or its subsidiary Crown Glass Manufacturing Company, including 272, 273, and 274. Copies of these catalog pages can be found in Margaret and Douglas Archer's *Imperial Glass*.

Documentation of all cuts done by Crown or perhaps at the factory is by no means complete, so it is not possible to conclude where a particular cut was added to a piece. Refer to Chapter 6 Additions to Lace Edge Pieces for a discussion of cuts after the pieces left the factory.

Lacking complete information, I have chosen to include all cut pieces in Chapter 5 Mould Number List and Pictures. To differentiate between cuts with unknown numbers, I have assigned Roman numerals. These are only for convenience and are not Imperial numbers, for the origin of the cuts is not known.

Identical moulds were necessary for popular pieces, because moulds became too hot for continuous use. They also wore out eventually and had to be replaced or retired. It makes economic sense that moulds not retired due to wear were sometimes brought back into service years later. Pieces in new colors appealed to customers, even if the moulds were old.

Examples of the reuse of older moulds are numerous. The earliest 745 pieces came in ten colors but reappeared in five more colors twenty years later. The 7455F 6 3/4" Shallow Nappy from the 1930s came back in the late 1950s as the 745F in Turquoise Opaque, Turquoise Doeskin Opaque, Burgundy, Heather, and Amberglo. The 7455B 6 1/2" Belled Nappy also came back but added crimping to become 745C in Milk Glass as well as the other five colors.

The Crocheted Crystal baskets made for Sears carried the Imperial 780 numbers and the Sears numbers 1723-25. About fifteen years later, Imperial produced the same baskets in Milk Glass and used the Sears numbers, even though the pieces were not made for Sears.

The punch bowl mould was another example of reuse over the years. Sears carried the punch bowl in every catalog containing Crocheted Crystal during the 1940s. In 1962, Imperial made a Purple Slag punch bowl and cups from the Crocheted Crystal moulds. Two years later, Imperial ran an ad for "Giant Size" salad bowls and showed the 13" Crystal punch bowl in the illustration.

120 7802K/cut 120: 3 1/2" Flower Bowl, Crystal, $18-21

Dates of Mould Usage

Moulds were very expensive to make. Former employees recall that it could take two years to go from an idea for a glass piece to a completed cast iron mould. Then a test period ran to determine whether production was feasible. Half a day's work, called a move or turn, was usually the minimum test period. If enough pieces could be produced to be cost-effective, the mould was put into regular production.

Shared Items

A few of the auxiliary pieces regularly included in Lace Edge or Crocheted Crystal sets did not originate as Lace Edge items. Imperial made these pieces for sets in other patterns as well. Chapter 5 Mould Number List and Pictures illustrates these pieces with the Lace Edge sets.

One example of a shared item is the 615 5" Ladle, rounded, which was used with the three types of Lace Edge mayonnaise sets. According to early catalogs, production of this ladle started in the 1920s. It was a common ladle used for other patterns, including Cape Cod, Washington, and Tradition. Another small ladle, the 169 5" Ladle (flat base) was not found with Lace Edge sets originally but sometimes is found in sets at stores now.

272 7802B/cut 272: 6" Bowl, Belled Shape, Crystal, $16-18

273 7801Z/cut 273: 4 1/2" Rose Bowl, Crystal, $32-35

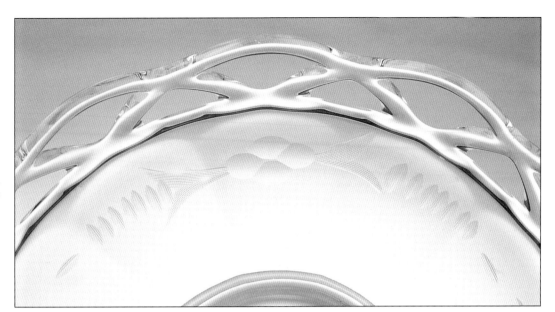

I 7806F/cut I: 8" Walnut Bowl,
Crystal, $23-26

II 7801S/cut II: 6" Square Bon Bon, 4-Toed, Crystal, $31-34

III 7805W/cut III: 5 1/2" Deep
Bowl, Crystal, $18-21

IV 7806C/cut IV: 7 3/4" Bowl,
Crimped, Crystal, $25-28

V 780/cut V: Sugar and Creamer Set, Crystal, $50-55

VI 7801W/cut VI: 7 1/2" Comport, 4-Toed, Crystal, $32-35

VII 7805B/cut VII: 5 1/2" Low Comporte, Crystal, $21-24

Other shared items were the 701 Fork and Spoon, sold as part of the Crocheted Crystal 7808/9 and 7808/9C Salad Sets. The fork and spoon reportedly were first made for the Reeded pattern, as indicated by the grooves running up the handles. Salad sets in Cape Cod, Mount Vernon, Washington, and perhaps other patterns used the 701.

The punch bowl ladles were also shared items. The 780 Punch Bowl Set in Purple Slag, produced only from July 1962 through December 1963, included the 780/91 Punch Ladle. This was the same ladle used with Candlewick, Mount Vernon, Washington, and other sets. More common for Lace Edge was the 703 Punch Ladle as part of the Crocheted Crystal 78010 Punch Bowl Set. There were no punch sets with the other Lace Edge mould number prefixes.

There is one item that originated as a Lace Edge piece and was later shared with other patterns. The 4 1/2" Twin Candleholder, produced in many colors, appeared on price lists for Mount Vernon and Washington and is often noted as being Mount Vernon. The mould number used on those price lists was the Lace Edge number 749 but eventually changed to a Washington number in later catalogs.

The Lace Edge collector who is familiar with the Imperial pattern Candlewick will notice the similarity between Candlewick beads and the beads used in the stems of 780 vases, compotes, and cake stand. There is no mistaking the lace edge, however, to identify the pieces as Lace Edge.

Logos and Labels

The only Imperial logo that was used on Lace Edge was the G with an I passing through it from top to bottom. Imperial started marking glass with this logo in 1951 and continued for twenty years. Most of the 1950 Milk Glass pieces in Lace Edge and several other colors manufactured during that time carry the IG logo. There are several labels still found on Lace Edge pieces that identify the items as Imperial, Belmont, or Crocheted Crystal. Other labels specify the mould number and color.

Imperial sticker – Hand Crafted

Imperial sticker – Hand Made Quality

Imperial IG logo

Belmont sticker – Belmont Crystal Hand Crafted

Crocheted Crystal sticker – Crocheted
Harmony House Hand Made Crystal

Imperial sticker and Color/mould number sticker –
Imperial 207K F(lower) / Arranger Verde

Backing of Crocheted Crystal sticker and Sears
Roebuck and Co. 6/1737 (Sears number) $2.49

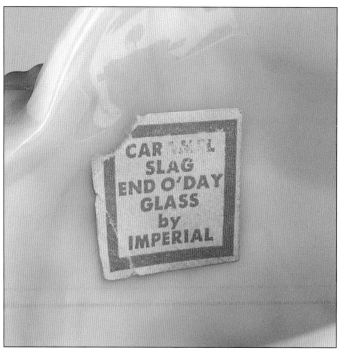

Slag sticker – Caramel Slag End o' Day Glass by Imperial

Chapter 4

Glass Colors

Lace Edge is a very colorful pattern. During the many years of Lace Edge production, Imperial used over forty colors. Because the company emphasized different colors at different times, colors can be used to estimate the date of manufacture. As an example, say you own a shallow nappy, which is about 6 to 6 1/2" wide and has an upright lace edge. The glass has a pattern of hexagons and squares. You know the approximate age of your piece, depending on the color, as follows:

1930s – pale Milk Glass, known by the color number 11/.
Late 1930s and early 1940s – Crystal, Stiegel Green, Ritz Blue, Amber, Imperial Green, Rose Pink, Ruby, Seafoam Blue, Seafoam Green.
1950s and 1960s – white Milk Glass (color number 1950/) and Doeskin (1952/), both known as 1950/ hereafter in this book.
Late 1950s – Turquoise Opaque, Turquoise Doeskin Opaque, Burgundy, Heather, Amberglo.

Some colors are so close to other colors as to be indistinguishable to the collector. Amber was made into Lace Edge glass in the late 1930s and early 1940s but reappeared in other Lace Edge pieces in the 1960s. At that time, a similar but slightly more yellow color called Flask Brown was being produced. Both colors appeared in Catalog 66A. Honey Amber dates to the late 1950s. Amberglo was pictured in Catalogs 69, 71R, and 73. Flask Brown and Honey Amber were not used on any Lace Edge pieces made in Amber. However, both Amber and Amberglo were used for the 78 Footed Bowl and Cover. Besides that piece, it may be easier to distinguish these three colors by knowing which pieces were made in which colors than by looking at the colors themselves.

Other examples of very close colors are Burgundy, Wistar Purple, and Heather. Burgundy is the darkest of the three, but the similarity is obvious. A common piece in Burgundy is the 207B, a number that appears in no extant Imperial documentation. Price Lists refer to 207C and 207F, but I have found neither of those pieces. Perhaps the C or F letter designation is a typographical error.

The same color can vary considerably from piece to piece, depending on the thickness of the glass and the manufacturing process. Ruby is the most variable because it was very difficult to manufacture consistently, due to its chemistry. The prices of ruby pieces were slightly more than other colors for the same pieces. The color of the glass can range from a red-orange to almost black. If an item looks black, you can hold it up to a light to see the red cast of the thinner parts of the glass pattern. Note that if you see purple instead, that piece is black amethyst, a color not used for Lace Edge. Ruby pieces that appear medium to dark red, but not black, often have a yellow cast in the thinner parts such as the base. This yellowing was the result of the reheating, or annealing, process during manufacture. Imperial sold such pieces not as seconds but as being a normal ruby color.

Today prices for the same type of piece often fluctuate by color. For example, collectors find that ruby pieces with no yellow have higher prices. Ritz Blue commands the elevated prices of many rich blue cobalt colors. Highest prices for certain items go for the Seafoam Blue and Seafoam Green versions, which can also be the hardest to find. Slag pieces sell for three or more times the price of similar pieces in single colors.

Imperial kept no all-inclusive lists stating the colors in which Lace Edge pieces were produced, or, if the corporation kept such lists, they no longer exist. My research has not found documented evidence of all known Imperial colors being made into Lace Edge pieces. For example, there is no Lace Edge in Jade Slag. The early Imperial catalogs were printed in black and white and usually did not mention available colors. Later catalogs showed colors, but not all production items ever appeared in a catalog. Salesmen's notebooks and price lists are good sources of information about what pieces were made in which colors.

Each of the pattern types appeared in a variety of colors. Although these group pictures do not represent all the Lace Edge colors, the wide array of light and dark is obvious. The collector can have hours of fun seeing how many colors of one piece she can find. Note the Amber as compared to the pale Amber 743B, an example of the variation within a color.

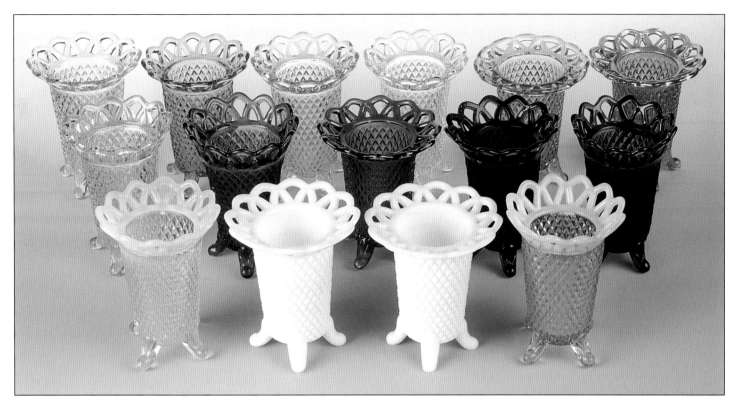

15 colors of 743B

10 colors of 7455B

3 colors of 749C

5 colors of 7497E (missing 2 known colors)

7 colors of 7801 pieces

Compiled from Imperial documents and pieces of Lace Edge, this list groups similar Lace Edge colors and shows their general dates of production. The pictures illustrate an example of each color. Three colors are not shown. Honey Amber and Midwest Rose were both used for only one piece, the 749C 7" Comporte. Mustard was used only for the 78 Footed Bowl and Cover. The collector who sees a 749C or a 78 can quickly know if she has found any of these missing colors by referring to Chapter 5 Mould Number List and Pictures for a complete list of colors used for each piece.

1930s-60s Crystal
1940s Satin (sandblasted Crystal)
1940s Pearl (Crystal with opalescent lace)
1930s-40s Milk Glass (11)
1950s-60s Milk Glass (1950)
1950s-60s Doeskin (1952) (sandblasted 1950 Milk Glass)
1950s-60s Turquoise Opaque
1950s-60s Turquoise Opaque Doeskin (sandblasted Turquoise Opaque)

1930s-50s Stiegel Green
1930s-40s Imperial Green
1930s-40s Seafoam Green
1940s-50s Green
1960s-70s Verde
1960s Olive

1930s-50s Ritz Blue
1930s-40s Seafoam Blue
1930s-40s Teal
1940s-50s Blue
1960s-70s Antique Blue
1960s Moonlight Blue

1930s-60s Amber
1950s-60s Flask Brown
1960s-70s Amberglo
1950s Honey Amber
1960s Honey
1960s Topaz
1960s Mustard
1960s Mandarin Gold

1930s-40s Rose Pink
1950s Midwest Rose
1960s-70s Azalea
1930s-50s Ruby
1940s-50s Flashed Ruby
1940s-50s Flashed Cranberry
1960s Decorated Ruby (same as Flashed Ruby)

1950s Wistar Purple
1950s Burgundy
1950s-60s Heather

1960s Rubigold Carnival
1960s Peacock Carnival
1960s Sunset Ruby Carnival

1960s-70s Purple Slag (Glossy)
1960s-70s Purple Slag (Satin)
1960s-70s Caramel Slag (Glossy)

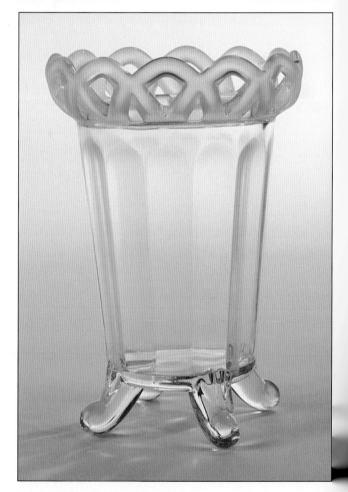

Satin 7455F: 6 3/4" Nappy, $21-24

Pearl 7803N: 5" Vase, 4-Toed, $22-25

Crystal 7802K: 3 1/2"
Flower Bowl, $14-16

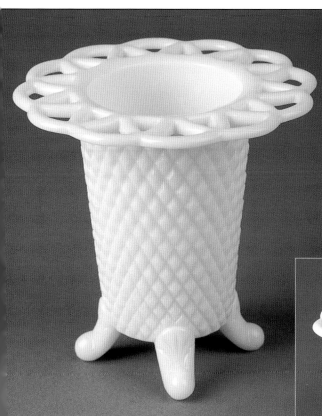

Doeskin (1952) 1950/220D: 12" Footed Cake Stand, $28-31

Milk Glass (11) 11/743X: 4 1/2"
Vase, 4-Toed, $22-25

Milk Glass (1950) 1950/220D: 12" Footed Cake Stand, $28-31

Turquoise Opaque 274C: 7" 4-Toed
Crimped Compote, $35-40

Turquoise Opaque Doeskin 274C: 274C: 7" 4-
Toed Crimped Compote, $35-40

Stiegel Green 7802D: 7 1/2" Plate, $14-16

Imperial Green 743B: 5 1/2"
Vase, 4-Toed, $28-31

Seafoam Green 749: 4 1/2" Candleholder, $200-210/pair

Green 7806F: 8" Walnut Bowl, $18-20

Verde 780: 6" Covered Bowl,
$35-40

Olive 7436: 7" Bowl (missing top), $15-18

Ritz Blue 7455G: 5"
Basket Bowl, $21-24

Seafoam Blue 7496D: 8" Salad Plate, $35-40. A speckled
variation of Seafoam Blue can also be found in the 745 pieces.

Teal 743N: 5 1/2" Vase, 4-Toed, $28-31

Blue 7801C: 7 1/2" Compote, 4-Toed, Crimped, $28-31

Antique Blue 78: Footed Bowl and Cover, $28-31

Amber 7801S: 6" Square Bon Bon, $28-31

Moonlight Blue 780: 6"
Covered Bowl, $35-40

Flask Brown 207K: 5" Flower Arranger with frog, $28-31

Amberglo 780: 6"
Covered Bowl, $35-40

Honcy 7136D: 9 1/2" Plate, $18-20

Topaz 7801W: 7 1/2"
Comport, 4-Toed, $28-31

Mandarin Gold 780: 6" Covered Bowl, $35-40

Rose Pink 7455B: 6 1/2" Belled Nappy, $21-24

Azalea 780: 6" Covered Bowl, $35-40

Ruby 7497E: 9 1/2" Basket Bowl, $28-31

Flashed Ruby 78C/754: 2-pc Epergne,
$160-170; flashed edge only

Flashed Cranberry 7804B: 5 1/2" Ftd. Jelly, $24-28

Wistar Purple 749C: 7" Crimped Compote, $28-31

Burgundy 207B: 7 3/4"
Bowl, $35-38

Heather 745C: 6" Crimped
Bowl, $14-16

Rubigold Carnival 749B: 6 1/2" Comporte, $32-35

Peacock Carnival 286B: 5"
Vase, 4-Toed, $32-35

Sunset Ruby Carnival 274C: 7" 4-Toed Crimped Compote, $40-45

Purple Slag (Satin) 780: 6"
Covered Bowl, $60-65

Purple Slag (Glossy) 780: 6" Covered Bowl, $60-65

Caramel Slag (Glossy) 78: Footed
Bowl and Cover, $115-125

Chapter 5

Mould Number List and Pictures

When Imperial reused a mould for a different color of glass, the assigned mould number was generally the same. This was true even if the same kind of mould was reused several years later. There were exceptions, however. One example was the 749 Sugar and Creamer Set made in the 1930s and 1940s. When the set appeared in Milk Glass in the 1950s and Caramel Slag in the 1960s, the number 30 was assigned. Another example was the use of the Sears catalog numbers for the Milk Glass baskets in the mid 1950s, after the Imperial numbers were used for the Crystal baskets sold at Sears in the 1940s.

The pictures in this chapter represent the shapes and sizes that were produced with the Lace Edge moulds. Each page lists the Catalogs (Cat), Salesman's Notebooks (SN), Price Lists (PL), or other sources (e.g. Photos - PH) where production of the piece by Imperial is documented. The list includes the printing dates, if they are known. One catalog offers only suggested dates – 1936(?) to 1940(?). Some documents cover many years and offer little help in proving the exact time of manufacture. A complete list of the documents represented appears in Chapter 7 Related Pieces by Imperial.

Lace Edge pieces known to exist but no longer found in print are labeled as "Undocumented," with a question mark after the mould number. By including these pieces in this chapter, I am expressing my confidence that they are Imperial's Lace Edge. I am also sure that collectors will find more Undocumented pieces in the future. This is the legacy of missing documentation.

Each entry shows the names used by Imperial. Names, including sizes, have not been changed to make them consistent but are shown as stated in the Imperial documentation. Information in parentheses is for clarification and was not written in Imperial documentation.

Many Imperial sources do not include notation about the colors in which pieces were created. One may wish to assume that if a bowl of a given size was made in two colors, the plate from the same mould probably was made in the same two colors. Without the proof of having all those pieces in hand, however, one cannot be sure this was the case. Therefore, each entry presents known colors and the catalogs in which they were noted.

If there is a question about a color's existence, that color is listed under "Other colors." Also noted there is the metallic coating added by Silvalyte after they bought the pieces from Imperial. Remember Imperial did not affix this coating. Refer to Chapter 6 Additions to Lace Edge Pieces for further explanation.

Imperial records show the dates for beginning and ending manufacture of slag pieces, many Milk Glass pieces, and some others. Where dates are known, they are included with each piece.

The collector can use this chapter to identify the pieces in her collection. Almost all sizes and shapes of Lace Edge are illustrated here. For a few items that lack pictures, the collector may be referred to a photograph showing another size of the same kind of piece. For others, unfortunately, I can only suggest the reader refer to Chapter 3 Understanding Mould Numbers. Prices in captions have been adjusted to reflect color and other factors mentioned in Chapter 9 Price List.

If any identification is not obvious, remember that the height and width of bowls and plates may vary slightly from processing. Bases stay the same. Refer to the section on Base Measurements in Chapter 3 Understanding Mould Numbers to verify the mould number.

743 series

743B: 5 1/2" Vase, 4-Toed, Rose Pink, $28-31

743B: 5 1/2" Vase, 4-Toed
Crystal, Stiegel Green, Ritz Blue, Amber, Rose Pink, Imperial Green,
Ruby
Cat 1936?-40?
Other colors: Seafoam Blue, Seafoam Green, Teal

11/743B: 5 1/4" Vase, 4-Toed
Milk Glass
Cat 1936?-40?

1950/286B: 5" Vase, 4-Toed
Milk Glass, Doeskin
Cat F-60, SN 57-58, Cat 57 Sup, PL 58, PL 61

286B
Rubigold Carnival, Peacock Carnival
Cat 64-65, Cat 66A, PH 69

7430B: 5 1/2" Vase, 4-Toed
Honey, Olive
PL 68, PH

743N: 5 1/2" Vase, 4-Toed, Imperial Green, $28-31

743N: 5 1/2" Vase, 4-Toed
Crystal, Stiegel Green, Ritz Blue, Amber, Rose Pink, Imperial Green,
Ruby
Cat 1936?-40?
Other colors: Seafoam Blue, Seafoam Green, and Teal

11/743N
Milk Glass
Cat 1936?-40?

743K: 5" Vase, 4-Toed, Ruby, $32-35

743K: 5" Vase, 4-Toed
Crystal, Stiegel Green, Ritz Blue, Amber, Rose Pink,
Imperial Green, Ruby
Cat 1936?-40?
Other colors: Seafoam Blue, Seafoam Green, and Teal

11/743K
Milk Glass
Cat 1936?-40?

743X: 4 1/2" Vase, 4-Toed,
Seafoam Blue, $35-38

743X: 4 1/2" Vase, 4-Toed
Crystal, Stiegel Green, Ritz
Blue, Amber, Rose Pink,
Imperial Green, Ruby
Cat 1936?-40?
Other colors: Seafoam Blue,
Seafoam Green, and Teal

11/743X
Milk Glass
Cat 1936?-40?

7432B: 7 3/4" Bowl, Ritz Blue, $35-38

7432B: 7 3/4" Bowl
Crystal
Cat 1936?-40?
Other colors: Stiegel Green, Ritz Blue, Amber, Rose Pink, Imperial
Green, Ruby, Seafoam Blue, Seafoam Green

207B
Burgundy
Undocumented

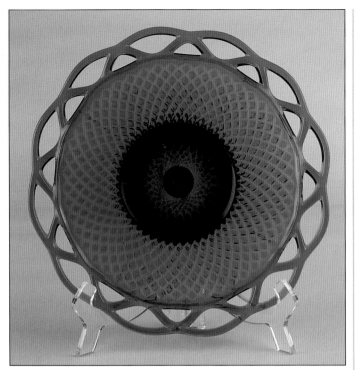

7432D: 9 1/2" Plate, Stiegel Green, $18-20

7435: 7" Bowl and Top, Olive, $28-31

7432D: 9 1/2" Plate
Crystal
Cat 1936?-40?
Other colors: Stiegel Green, Ritz Blue, Amber, Rose Pink, Imperial
Green, Ruby, Seafoam Blue, Seafoam Green

7432/86: Tid Bit Set – 12" and 9 1/2" Plates
Crystal
Cat 1936?-40?

7435: 7" Bowl and Top
Honey, Olive
PL 68, PH

7432F: 8" Shallow Nappy, Topaz, $22-25

7432F: 8" Shallow Nappy
Crystal
Cat 1936?-40?
Other colors: Stiegel Green, Ritz Blue, Amber, Rose Pink, Imperial
Green, Ruby, Seafoam Blue, Seafoam Green, Topaz

274C: 7" 4-Toed Crimped Compote, Purple Slag, $50-55

7436: 7" Bowl and Top, Honey, $22-25

7435C: 7" 4-Toed Crimped Compote
Honey, Olive
PL 68, PH

1950/274C: 7" 4-Toed Compote
Milk Glass / Doeskin
Cat C-53, Cat D-mid 50s, Cat E-Late 50s, Cat F-60, SN 57-58,
Cat 57 Sup, PL 58, SN 39-63, PH 65

274C: 7" 4-Toed Crimped Compote
Heather
SN 53-5, SN 57-58, PL 58

274C
Turquoise, Turquoise Doeskin
PH 55-58, SN 57-58, PL 58
Discontinued 1/1/68

274C
Burgundy
PL 59, PH 53-59

274C
Purple Slag
Cat 62, PL 63, Cat 66A,
PH 62-64
Discontinued 12/31/67
or 1/1/68

274C
Sunset Ruby Carnival
PL 68, PL 69

7436: 7" Bowl and Top
Honey, Olive
PL 68, PH

7436/5B: 7 3/4" Bowl, Crystal, $22-25

7436/5B: 7 3/4" Bowl (Intaglio Roses)
Crystal
Cat 1936?-40?, PL 41, PL 38-42, SN 45-46
Discontinued 1/1/46

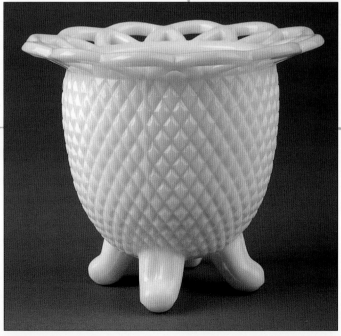

1950/274K: 5 1/2" 4-Toed Compote, Milk Glass, $28-31

1950/274K: 5 1/2" 4-Toed Compote
Milk Glass
PH (no date)

7436/5C: 7 3/4" Bowl, Crimped, Crystal, $25-28

1950/B207C: 7 1/2" Crimped Bowl on Brass Base, Milk Glass, $35-40

7436/5C: 7 3/4" Bowl, Crimped (Intaglio Roses)
Crystal
Cat/PL 40s-50s

7436C: 7 1/2" Crimped Bowl
Honey, Olive
PL 68, PH

207C
Burgundy
PH 53-59, PL 59

1950/207C
Milk Glass, Doeskin
Cat C-53, Cat D-mid 50s, Cat E-late 50s, Cat F-60,
SN 57-58, PL 58, PL 59, PL 61, PH 65

1950/B207C: 7 1/2" Crimped Bowl on Brass Base
Milk Glass, Doeskin
PH 53-57, SN 57-58

7436D: 9 1/2" Plate, Olive, $18-20

7436/5D: 9 1/2" Plate (Intaglio Roses)
Crystal
Cat 1936?-40?, Cat/PL 40s-50s, PL 41, PL 38-42, SN 45-46
Discontinued 1/1/46

7436D: 9 1/2" Plate
Honey, Olive
PL 68, PH

7436F: 8" Bowl, Shallow, Olive, $18-20

63

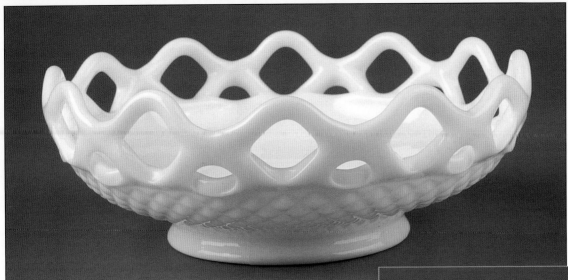

1950/207F: 8" Bowl, Shallow, Milk Glass, $22-25

7436/5F: 8" Nappy (Intaglio Roses)
Crystal
Cat 1936?-40?, Cat/PL 40s-50s, PL 41, PL 38-42

7436F: 8" Bowl, Shallow
Honey, Olive
PL 68, PH

207F
Burgundy
PH 53-59, PL 59

1950/207F
Milk Glass, Doeskin
Cat C-53, Cat D-mid 50s, Cat E-late 50s, Cat F-60, Cat 57 Sup, SN 57-58, PL 58, PL 59, PL 61, PH 65

1950/207K: 5" Flower Arranger, Milk Glass, $14-16

7436K: 5" Flower Arranger
Honey, Olive
PL 68, PH

207K: 5" Flower Arranger (with or without frog)
Verde, Heather, Flask Brown
Cat 62
Verde, Antique Blue, Flask Brown
PL 63, Cat 66A, SN 67-68
Verde, Antique Blue, Amberglo
PL 68

1950/207K
Milk Glass, Doeskin
Cat 62, PH 64, Cat 66A, SN 67-68, PL 68

207K: 5" Flower Arranger, Antique Blue, $28-31

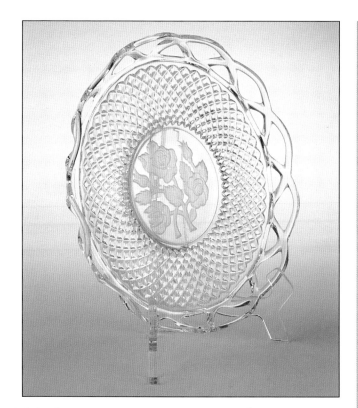

7436/5V(?): 8 1/2" Plate, Upturned Edge, Crystal, $28-31

7436/5V(?): 8 1/2" Plate, Upturned Edge (Intaglio Roses)
Crystal
Undocumented

7436/5X: 8" Bowl, Flanged Edge, Crystal, $28-31

7436/5X: 8" Bowl, Flanged Edge (Intaglio Roses)
Crystal
Cat 1936?-40?

745: Ivy Ball (no chain), Rose Pink, $14-16

745: Ivy Ball with Chain
Crystal
Cat 1936?-40?
Other colors: Stiegel Green, Ritz Blue, Amber, Rose Pink, Imperial
Green, Ruby, Seafoam Blue, Seafoam Green

745(?): Ivy Ball (Upright), Stiegel Green, $28-31

745(?): Ivy Ball (Upright)
Stiegel Green, Ritz Blue, Amber, Rose Pink, Imperial Green, Ruby
Undocumented

7455B: 6 1/2" Belled Nappy, Ritz Blue, $21-24

7455B: 6 1/2" Belled Nappy
Crystal, Stiegel Green, Ritz Blue, Amber, Rose Pink, Imperial Green,
Ruby
Cat 1936?-40?
Crystal
Cat/PL 40s-50s
Other colors: Seafoam Blue, Seafoam Green

7455B(?): 6 1/2" Belled Nappy (Bellaire Centennial)
Crystal
Undocumented

11/7455B: 6 1/2" Belled Nappy
Milk Glass
Cat 1936?-40?

745C(?): 6" Crimped Bowl, Flask Brown, $14-16

745C: 6" Crimped Bowl, Turquoise, $14-16

745C: 6" Crimped Bowl
Turquoise, Turquoise Doeskin
PH 55-58, SN 57-58, PL 58

745C
Burgundy
PH 53-59

745C
Heather
SN 54, SN 57-58, PL 58

745C(?)
Flask Brown
Undocumented

1950/745C
Milk Glass, Doeskin
Cat C-53, Cat D-mid 50s, Cat E-late 50s, Cat F-60, SN 57-58, PL 58,
PL 59, Cat 66A, PH 64, PH 65
Discontinued 1/1/68

Imperial logo on base of 745C, although
bowl is Undocumented

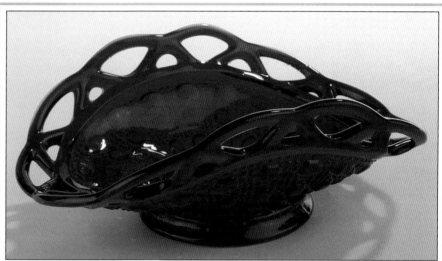

745E(?): 7" Basket Bowl, Ruby, $28-31

745E(?): 7" Basket Bowl
Ruby
Undocumented

7455D: 7 1/2" Plate, Crystal, $14-16

7455D: 7 1/2" Plate
Crystal, Stiegel Green, Ritz Blue, Amber, Rose Pink, Imperial Green,
Ruby
Cat 1936?-40?
Crystal
Cat/PL 40s-50s
Other colors: Seafoam Blue, Seafoam Green

7455D(?): 7 1/2" Plate (Bellaire Centennial)
Crystal
Undocumented

11/7455D: 7 1/2" Plate
Milk Glass
Cat 1936?-40?

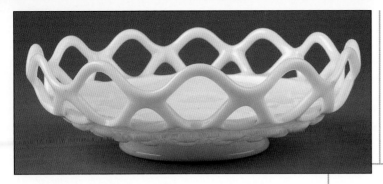

11/7455F: 6 3/4" Shallow Nappy, Milk Glass, $18-20

7455F: 6 3/4" Nappy
Crystal, Stiegel Green, Ritz Blue, Amber, Rose Pink, Imperial
Green, Ruby
Cat 1936?-40?
Crystal
PL 38-42, Cat/PL 40s-50s
Other colors: Seafoam Blue, Seafoam Green

7455F (?): 6 3/4" Nappy (Bellaire Centennial)
Crystal
Undocumented

11/7455F: 6 3/4" Shallow Nappy
Milk Glass
Cat 1936?-40?

745F: 6" Shallow Bowl
Turquoise, Turquoise Doeskin
PH 55-58, SN 57-58, PL 58

745F
Burgundy
PH 53-59

745F
Heather
SN 54, SN 57-58, PL 58

745F(?)
Flask Brown
Undocumented

1950/745F: 6" Bowl (Shallow)
Milk Glass, Doeskin
Cat C-53, Cat D-mid 50s, Cat E-late 50s, Cat F-60, SN 57-
58, PL 58, PL 59, PH 65
Discontinued 1/1/68

749: 4 1/2" Candleholder, Blue, $28-31/pair

749: 4 1/2" Candleholder (Twin)
Crystal
Cat 36?-40?, PL 41, PL 38-42, SN 45-46, PH 38 et al
Other colors: Stiegel Green, Ritz Blue, Amber, Rose Pink, Imperial
Green, Ruby, Seafoam Blue, Seafoam Green, Blue

7490
Honey, Olive
PL 68, PH

1950/279: Twin Candleholder
Milk Glass, Doeskin
Cat F-60, SN 57-58, Cat 57 Sup

7455G: 5" Basket Bowl, Rose Pink, $18-20

7455G: 5" Basket Bowl
Crystal, Stiegel Green, Ritz Blue, Amber, Rose Pink,
Imperial Green, Ruby
Cat 1936?-40?
Other colors: Seafoam Blue, Seafoam Green

11/7455G: 6" Basket Bowl or Jardinière
Milk Glass
Cat 1936?-40?

30: Sugar and Creamer Set, Caramel Slag (Glossy), $70-75

749: Sugar and Creamer Set
Crystal
Cat 36?-40?, PL 38-42
Other colors: Seafoam Blue, Seafoam Green

1950/30
Milk Glass / Doeskin
Cat D-mid 50s, Cat E-late 50s, SN 57-58, PL 58, PL 59, PL 61
Began production 1/1/55; doeskin discontinued 1/1/68

30
Caramel Slag (Glossy only)
Cat 66A, Cat 69, PL 69, Cat 71R
Began production 7/1/64; discontinued 12/31/70

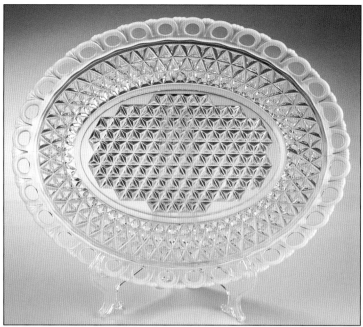

749: 13" Oval Platter, Seafoam Green, $170-180

749: 13" Oval Platter
Crystal
Cat 36?-40?
Other colors: Seafoam Blue, Seafoam Green

749: Cup and Saucer, Seafoam Blue, $60-65

749: Cup and Saucer
Crystal
Cat 36?-40?
Other colors: Seafoam Blue, Seafoam Green

749: 9 ounce Tumbler, Seafoam Blue, $50-55

749: 9 ounce Tumbler
Crystal
Cat 36?-40?, PL 38-42
Other colors: Seafoam Blue, Seafoam Green

749B: 6 1/2" Comporte, Peacock Carnival, $35-38

749C: 3-pc Mayonnaise Set, Seafoam Green, $170-180

749B: 6 1/2" (or 7") Comporte
Rubigold Carnival, Peacock Carnival
Cat 64-65, Cat 66A, PH 65

1950/749B: 7" Comporte
Milk Glass, Doeskin
Cat C-53, Cat D-mid 50s, Cat E-late 50s, Cat F-60, SN 57-58, PL 58, PL 59, PL 61
Began production 1/1/54

749C: 3-pc Mayonnaise Set
Crystal
Cat 36?-40?
Other colors: Seafoam Blue, Seafoam Green

749C: 7" Comporte, Stiegel Green, $28-31

1950/749F: 7" Comporte, Milk Glass, $14-16

749C: 7" Comporte
Honey Amber, Midwest Rose, Stiegel Green, Wistar Purple
SN 57-58, Cat 57 Sup, PL 58, PH (no date)

749C
Burgundy
PH 53-59

1950/749F: 7" Comporte
Milk Glass, Doeskin
Cat C-53, Cat D-mid 50s, Cat E-late 50s, Cat F-60, SN 57-58, Cat 57

Sup, PL 58, PL 59, PL 61
Began production 1/1/54

1950/749F: 7" Comporte/Brass Handle Server
Milk Glass, Doeskin
Cat 61Sup One, PH 62

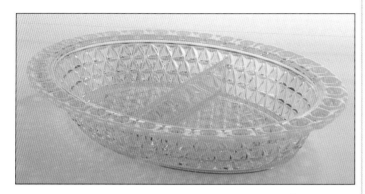

749/2: 11" Oval Divided Vegetable Bowl, Seafoam Green, $190-200

749/1: 11" Oval Vegetable Bowl
Crystal
Cat 36?-40?
Other colors: Seafoam Blue, Seafoam Green

749/2: 11" Oval Divided Vegetable Bowl
Crystal
Cat 36?-40?
Other colors: Seafoam Blue, Seafoam Green

7494X: 4 1/2" Fruit, Seafoam Blue, $28-31

7494X: 4 1/2" Fruit
Crystal
Cat 36?-40?
Other colors: Seafoam Blue, Seafoam Green

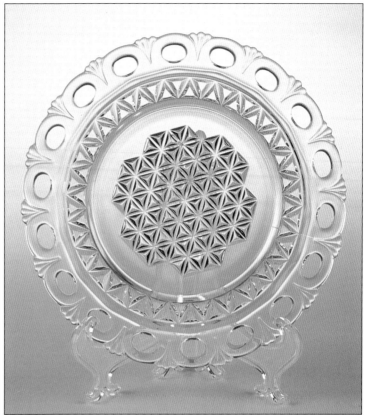

7495D: 6 1/2" Bread and Butter Plate, Crystal, $2-4

7495D: 6 1/2" Bread and Butter Plate
Crystal
Cat 36?-40?
Other colors: Seafoam Blue, Seafoam Green

7495W(?): 5 1/2" Cereal Bowl, Seafoam Blue, $35-40

7495W(?): 5 1/2" Cereal Bowl
Crystal, Seafoam Blue, Seafoam Green
Undocumented

71

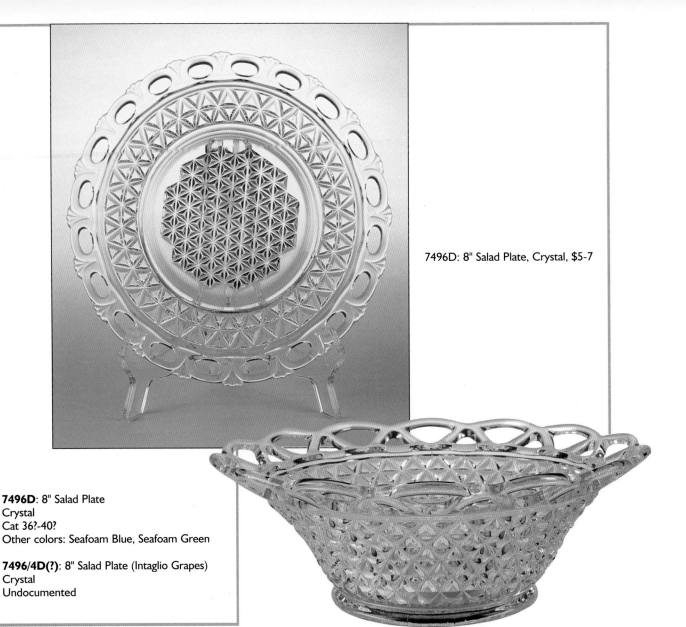

7496D: 8" Salad Plate, Crystal, $5-7

7496D: 8" Salad Plate
Crystal
Cat 36?-40?
Other colors: Seafoam Blue, Seafoam Green

7496/4D(?): 8" Salad Plate (Intaglio Grapes)
Crystal
Undocumented

7497B: 9" Bowl, Crystal, $28-31

7497B: 9" Bowl (Belled)
Crystal
Cat 1936?-40?, PL 38-42
Other colors: Stiegel Green, Ritz Blue, Amber, Ruby, Seafoam Blue, Seafoam Green

7497B: 3-pc Console – 9" Bowl, Twin Candleholders (749)
Crystal
Cat 1936?-40?, PL 41

7497/3B: 8 1/2" Belled Bowl (Intaglio Apple and Pear)
Crystal
Cat 1936?-40?, PL 41, SN 45-46
Discontinued 1/1/46

7498D/7498B: 2-pc Salad Set – 9" Bowl, 12" Plate
Crystal
Cat 1936?-40?

7497/3C: 8 1/2" Crimped Bowl (Intaglio Apple and Pear) (*Not pictured*)
Crystal
Cat 1936?-40?, Cat/PL 40s-50s

7496/4W(?): 7" Soup Bowl, Flared, Crystal, $5-7

7496W: 7" Soup Bowl, Flared
Crystal
Cat 36?-40?
Other colors: Seafoam Blue, Seafoam Green

7496/4W(?): 7" Soup Bowl, Flared (Intaglio Grapes)
Crystal
Undocumented

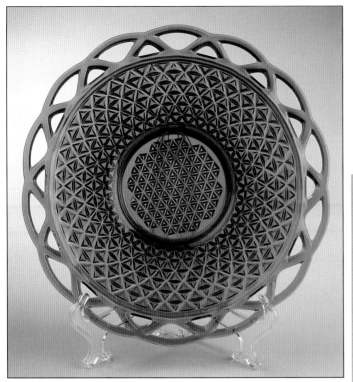

7497D: 11" Plate, Amber, $18-20

7497D: 11" Plate
Crystal
Cat 1936?-40?, PL 38-42
Other colors: Stiegel Green, Ritz Blue, Amber, Ruby, Seafoam Blue, Seafoam Green

7497D
Honey, Olive
PL 68, PH

7497/3D: 11" Plate (Intaglio Apple and Pear)
Crystal
Cat 1936?-40?, PL 38-42, Cat/PL 40s-50s, PL 41, SN 45-46
Discontinued 1/1/46

7497F: 9 1/2" Bowl, Shallow, Crystal, $18-20

7497F: 9 1/2" Bowl, Shallow
Crystal
Cat 1936?-40?, PL 38-42
Other colors: Stiegel Green, Ritz Blue, Amber, Ruby, Seafoam Blue, Seafoam Green

7497F: 3-pc Console - 9 1/2" Bowl, Twin Candleholders (749)
Crystal
Cat 1936?-40?, PL 38-42, PL 41

7497F: 9" Bowl, Shallow
Honey, Olive
PL 68, PH

7497/3F: 9" Bowl, Shallow (Intaglio Apple and Pear)
Crystal
Cat 1936?-40?, PL 38-42, Cat/PL 40s-50s, PL 41, SN 45-46

7497E: 9 1/2" Basket Bowl, Ritz Blue, $60-65

7497E: 9 1/2" Basket Bowl
Crystal
Cat 1936?-40?
Other colors: Stiegel Green, Ritz Blue, Amber, Ruby, Seafoam Blue, Seafoam Green

7497K: 6 1/2" Rose Bowl and Holder, Blue, $28-31

7497K: 6 1/2" Rose Bowl and Holder (metal)
Crystal
Cat 1936?-40?
Other colors: Blue, Verde

7497N: 6 1/2" Flower Bowl (*Not pictured*)
Crystal
Cat 1936?-40?

7498B: 10" Bowl, Belled, Stiegel Green, $35-40

7498B: 10" Bowl, Belled
Crystal
Cat 1936?-40?, PL 38-42
Other colors: Stiegel Green, Ritz Blue, Amber, Ruby, Seafoam Blue, Seafoam Green, Blue

7498B: 3-pc Console – 10" Bowl, Belled, Twin Candleholders (749)
Crystal
Cat 1936?-40?, PL 41

7498/4B: 10" Bowl, Belled (Intaglio Grapes)
Crystal
SN 45-46, PH (no date)
Discontinued 1/1/46

7498/4B: 3-pc Console – 10" Bowl (Intaglio Grapes), Twin Candleholders (749)
Crystal
SN 45-46

7497R: 6 1/2" Flower Bowl and Holder,
Crystal, $28-31

7497R: 6 1/2" Flower Bowl and Holder (metal)
Crystal
Cat 1936?-40?

74

7498B: 3-pc Console, Crystal, $55-60

7499D/7498B: 2-pc Salad Set – 10" Bowl, 14" Plate
Crystal
Cat 1936?-40?

7498/4C: 10" Crimped Bowl (Intaglio Grapes) (*Not pictured*)
Crystal
Cat/PL 40s-50s

7498D: 12" Plate
Crystal
Cat 1936?-40?, PL 38-42
 Other colors: Stiegel Green, Ritz Blue, Amber, Ruby,
  Seafoam Blue, Seafoam Green, Blue

7498/4D: 12" Plate (Intaglio Grapes)
 Crystal
 SN 45-46, Cat/PL 40s-50s
 Discontinued 1/1/46

749/1: 5-pc Ensemble – 12" Plate, 6
 1/2" Rose Bowl and Holder
 (7497K), Twin Candleholders
 (749)
  Crystal
  Cat 1936?-40?

7498D: Cheese and Cracker
 Set (12" Plate with 6 1/4"
 Birch Wood Center)
 Crystal
 Cat 1936?-40?

7498/97: Tid Bit Set – 12" and
 11" Plates
 Crystal
 Cat 1936?-40?

1950/275D: 12" Plate
 Milk Glass, Doeskin
 PH (no date)
 Discontinued 66

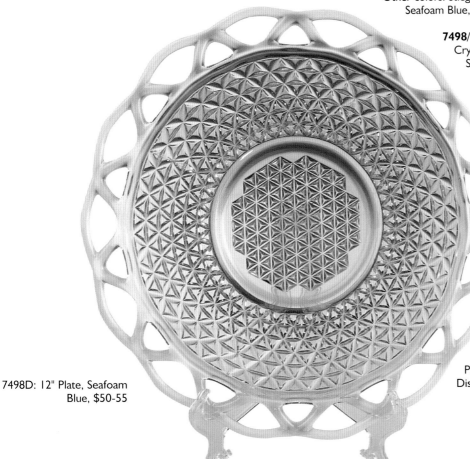

7498D: 12" Plate, Seafoam
Blue, $50-55

7498F: 11" Bowl, Shallow, Amber, $18-20

7498F: 3-pc. Console, Crystal, $40-45

7498K: 7 1/2" Rose Bowl and Holder, Verde, $35-40

7498F: 11" Bowl, Shallow
Crystal
Cat 1936?-40?, PL 38-42
Other colors: Stiegel Green, Ritz Blue, Amber, Ruby, Seafoam Blue,
Seafoam Green, Blue

7498F: 3-pc Console – 11" Bowl, Twin Candleholders (749)
Crystal
Cat 1936?-40?, PL 41, PL 38-42

7498/4F(?): 11" Bowl, Shallow (Intaglio Grapes)
Crystal
Undocumented

1950/275F: 10" Bowl
Milk Glass, Doeskin
Cat D-mid 50s, Cat E-late 50s, Cat F-60, SN 57-58, PL 58, PL 61, PH 65

7498K: 7 1/2" Rose Bowl and Holder (metal)
Crystal
Cat 1936?-40?, PL 41
Other colors: Verde

7498N: 7 1/2" Flower Bowl (*Not pictured*)
Crystal
Cat 1936?-40?

7498R: 6 1/2" Flower Bowl and Holder (metal) (*Not pictured; Compare 7497R*)
Crystal
Cat 1936?-40?

7499B: 12" Orange Bowl,
Crystal, $50-55

7499B: 12" Orange Bowl
Crystal
Cat 1936?-40?
Other colors: Amber, Blue

7499B: 3-pc Console – 12" Bowl, Twin Candleholders (749)
Crystal
Cat 1936?-40?, PL 41

7499/4B: 12" Orange Bowl (Intaglio Grapes)
Crystal
Cat 1936?-40?, Cat/PL 40s-50s, PL 41, SN 45-46
Discontinued 1/1/46

7499D
Honey, Olive
PL 68, PH

7499/4D: 14" Plate (Intaglio Grapes)
Crystal
Cat 1936?-40?, Cat/PL 40s-50s, PL 41, SN 45-46
Discontinued 1/1/46

749/2: 5-pc Ensemble – 14" Plate, 7 1/2" Rose Bowl and Holder
(7498K), Twin Candleholders (749)
Crystal
Cat 1936?-40?

7497/9: Tid Bit Set – 14" and 11" Plates
Honey, Olive
PL 68, PH

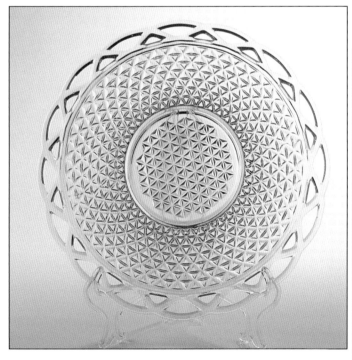

7499D: 14" Plate, Blue, $22-25

7499D: 14" Plate
Crystal
Cat 1936?-40?, PL 38-42
Other colors: Amber, Blue

7499/4F: 13" Fruit Bowl, Crystal, $40-45

7499F: 13" Fruit Bowl
Crystal
Cat 1936?-40?, PL 38-42
Other colors: Amber, Blue

7499F: 3-pc Console – 13" Bowl, Twin Candleholders (749)
Crystal
Cat 1936?-40?, PL 38-42, PL 41

7499F: 11 1/2" Fruit Bowl
Honey, Olive
PL 68, PH

7499/4F: 13" Fruit Bowl (Intaglio Grapes)
Crystal
Cat 1936?-40?, PL 38-42, Cat/PL 40s-50s, PL 41
Other colors: Amber, Blue

7499N: 8 1/2" Flower Bowl (*Not pictured*)
Crystal
Cat 1936?-40?

7499V: 13" Torte Plate (*Not pictured*)
Crystal
Cat 1936?-40?, PL 38-42

7499/4V: 13" Cabaret Plate
Crystal
Cat 1936?-40?

74910X: 9" Round Vegetable, Seafoam Green, $190-200

74910X: 9" Round Vegetable
Crystal
Cat 36?-40?
Other colors: Seafoam Blue, Seafoam Green

1950/715: Pie Server (*Not pictured*)
Milk Glass, Doeskin
Cat C-53, PH (no date)
Began production 1954

1950/220C: 10" Footed Crimped Bowl (*Not pictured*)
Milk Glass, Doeskin
Cat E-late 50s, Cat 57 Sup, PL 58, PL 59, PL 61

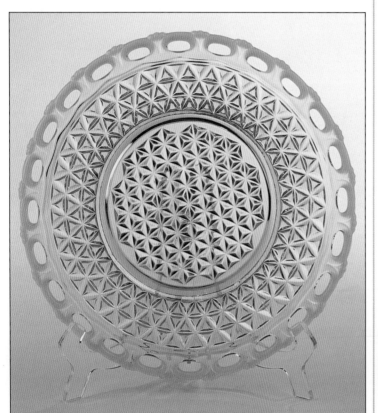

74910D: 10" Dinner Plate, Seafoam Blue, $150-160

74910D: 10" Dinner Plate
Crystal
Cat 36?-40?
Other colors: Seafoam Blue, Seafoam Green

7410/6: Tid Bit Set – 10" and 8" Plates
Crystal
Cat 36?-40?
Other colors: Seafoam Blue, Seafoam Green

220D: 12" Footed Cake Stand, Crystal, $70-75

220D: 12" Footed Cake Stand
Crystal
SN 53

1950/220D: 12" Footed Cake Stand
Milk Glass, Doeskin
Cat/PL 40s-50s, Cat B-52, Cat C-53, Cat D-mid 50s, Cat E-late 50s, Cat F-60, SN 53, Cat 57 Sup, SN 57-58, PL 58, PL 61, PH 65, Cat 66A, Cat 69A, PH 69

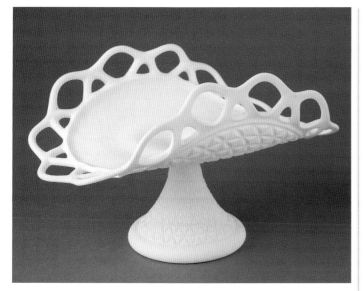

1950/220E: 12" Footed Banana Stand or Bowl, Doeskin, $50-55

1950/220E: 12" Footed Banana Stand or Bowl
Milk Glass, Doeskin
Cat B-52, Cat D-mid 50s, Cat E-late 50s, Cat F-60, SN 53, Cat 57 Sup,
SN 57-58, PL 58, PL 61, Cat 66A
Discontinued 1/1/68

78: Footed Bowl and Cover, Verde, $28-31

78: Footed Bowl and Cover (9 1/2")
Verde, Antique Blue, Mustard, Heather
Cat 62 Sup One
Verde, Antique Blue, Amber
Cat 66A
Verde, Amberglo
Cat 69, Cat 71R
Other documents: SN 67-68, PL 4/15/73

78: Footed Bowl and Cover (9 1/2")
Caramel Slag (Glossy only)
Cat 66A
Discontinued 1/1/68

1950/78: 9 1/2" Footed Jar
Milk Glass, Doeskin
Cat 62 Sup One

1950/220F: 10" Footed Fruit Bowl, Milk Glass, $28-31

1950/220F: 10" Footed Fruit Bowl
Milk Glass, Doeskin
Cat B-52, Cat D-mid 50s, Cat E-late 50s, Cat F-60, SN 53, Cat 57 Sup,
SN 57-58, PL 58, PL 61, PH 65, Cat 66A, SN 67-68, Cat 69A, PH 69

1950/220X: 9 1/2" Footed Bowl (*Not pictured*)
Milk Glass, Doeskin
Cat B-52

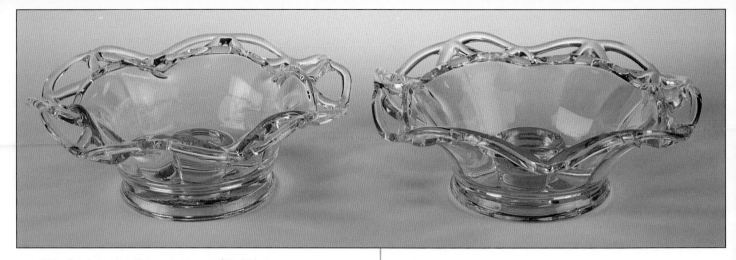

78C: Candleholder Crimped, Crystal, $28-31/pair

1950/78C: 6" Candleholder, Milk Glass, $22-25/pair

78C: Candleholder Crimped (same as 7802C Saucer Candle)
Crystal
Cat/PL 40s-50s, PL 41, PL 6/29/49, SN 39-63, PH 43-50, SN 54-55
Other color: aftermarket silvery coating

78C/cut 120: Candleholder Crimped
Crystal
PL 41

780C: Hurricane Lamps (for Candleholder Crimped)
Crystal
SN 39-63, PH 43-50

7802: 2-pc Hurricane Lamp (7802C, 780C)
Crystal
SN 39-63

1950/78C: 6" Candleholder
Milk Glass, Doeskin
Cat D-mid 50s, Cat E-late 50s, SN 57-58, PL 58, Cat 59, PL 61

78C/754: 2-pc Epergne, Crystal, $140-150

78C/754: 2-pc Epergne (Candleholder base)
Crystal
Cat/PL 40s-50s, PL 41
Other color: Flashed Ruby Edge

78K: Candleholder, Crystal, $28-31/pair

78K: Candleholder
Crystal
Cat/PL 40s-50s, PL 41, PL 38-42, SN 54-55
Other color: aftermarket silvery coating

78K/cut 120
Crystal
PL 38-42

78K/cut 272
Crystal
SN 39-63

Irice #M-80: Lace Edge Clock Face
Crystal
Imperial file quoted in Garrisons' *Imperial Boudoir, Etcetera…*

Irice #M-163: 7" Stand Mirror Frame
Crystal
1943-1945
Imperial file quoted in Garrisons' *Imperial Boudoir, Etcetera…*

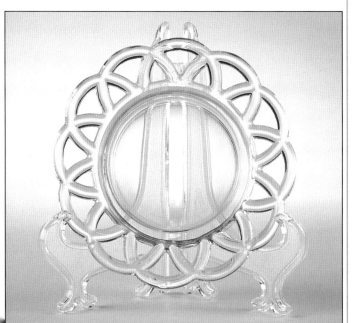

780(?): Lace Edge Coaster, Crystal, $40-45

780(?): Lace Edge Coaster (Used for Irice Clock)
Crystal
Undocumented

780: 4 1/2" Candleholder, Crystal, $18-20/pair

780: 4 1/2" Candleholder (Twin)
Crystal
Cat/PL 40s-50s, PL 41, PL 38-42, SN 45-46, PL 6/29/49, PH 43-50, SN 54-55

780: 6" Covered Bowl, Heather, $35-40

780: 6" Covered Bowl (base – clear)
Verde, Heather, Moonlight Blue, Mandarin Gold
Cat 62, PL 63

780: 6" Covered Bowl (base – IG)
Verde, Antique Blue, Azalea
Cat 66A
Verde, Antique Blue, Azalea, Amberglo
SN 67-68, Cat 69, PL 69
Rubigold Carnival, Peacock Carnival
Undocumented

780: 6" Covered Bowl (base – atom)
Verde, Antique Blue, Azalea, Amberglo
Cat 71R

780: 6" Covered Bowl (cover – mould number 170)
Purple Slag (Glossy only)
Cat 62, PH 64, Cat 66, Cat 66A, SN 67-68, Cat 71R
Glossy began production 1/1/62

780
Purple Slag (Glossy and Satin)
PL 73
Satin began production 1/1/73
Glossy and Satin discontinued 12/31/73

780/Dec: 6" Covered Bowl "Sweet Server"
Decorated Ruby (Flashed Ruby)
Cat 62 Sup One

780: Oyster Cocktail (*Not pictured; compare 780 below*)
Crystal
PL 38-42, PL 6/29/49, PH 43-50

780: 5 1/2 oz. Ftd Juice Tumbler (*Not pictured; compare 780 below*)
Crystal
PL 38-42, PL 6/29/49, PH 43-50

780: 3 1/2 oz. Cocktail (*Not pictured; compare 780 below*)
Crystal
PL 38-42, PL 6/29/49, PH 43-50

780: 4 1/2 oz. Claret Wine, Crystal, $40-45

Detail of Claret
showing Lace Edge

780: 4 1/2 oz. Claret Wine
Crystal
PL 38-42, PL 6/29/49, PH 43-50

780: 12 oz. Ftd Ice Tea (*Not pictured; compare 780 below*)
Crystal
PL 38-42, PL 6/29/49, PH 43-50

780: 5 1/2 oz. Tall Sherbet, Crystal, $40-45

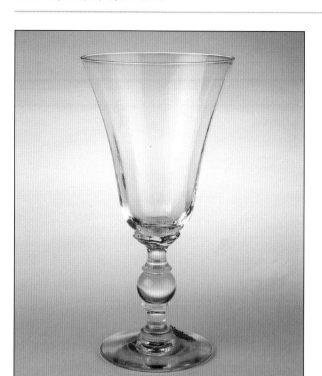

780: 10 oz. Goblet, Crystal, $60-65

Detail of Goblet showing Lace Edge

780: 10 oz. Goblet
Crystal
PL 38-42, PL 6/29/49, PH 43-50

Detail of Sherbet showing Lace Edge

780: 5 1/2 oz. Tall Sherbet
Crystal
PL 38-42, PL 6/29/49, PH 43-50

780(?): Low Compote, Crystal, $22-25

780(?): Low Compote
Crystal
Undocumented

780: Sugar and Creamer – new style, Crystal, $35-40

780: Sugar and Creamer – new style
Crystal
PL 38-42, PL 6/29/49, PH 43-50

1950/790: Sugar and Creamer Set
Milk Glass, Doeskin
Cat D-mid 50s, SN 57-58
Discontinued 1/1/58

1950/B790: Sugar and Creamer Set, brass base
Milk Glass, Doeskin
PH 53-57, SN 57-58

780: Sugar and Creamer – old style, Crystal, $40-45

780: Sugar and Creamer – old style
Crystal
PL 38-42, PH 43-50

780/cut 273: Sugar and Creamer – old style
Crystal
PL 38-42

780(?)/cut V: Sugar and Creamer – old style
Crystal
Undocumented

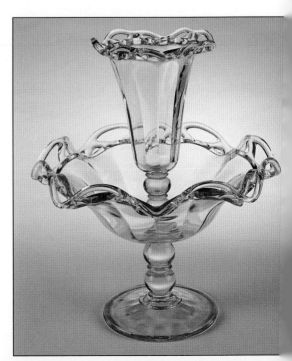

780C: 2-pc Epergne,
Crystal, $170-180

780C: 2-pc Epergne
Crystal
SN 39-63

780: Epergne Vase
Crystal
SN 39-63

780C: Epergne Bowl
Crystal
SN 39-63

780D: 12 1/2" Cake Stand, Crystal, $40-45

780D: 12 1/2" Cake Stand
Crystal
SN 39-63, PL 6/29/49, PH 43-50, SN 54-55

780F: 10" Ftd. Fruit Stand, Crystal, $35-40

780D: 10" Ftd. Fruit Stand
Crystal
PL 6/29/49, PH 43-50, SN 54-55

7800: 3-pc Mayonnaise Set, Crystal, $35-40

7800: 3-pc Mayonnaise Set – 7 1/2" Plate (7802D), 5" Bowl (780),
5" Ladle (615)
Crystal
PL 38-42, SN 39-63, PL 6/29/49, PH 43-50, SN 54-55

780: 5" Bowl (Mayonnaise Set)
Crystal
SN 39-63

615: 5" Ladle (rounded)
Crystal
PL 38-42

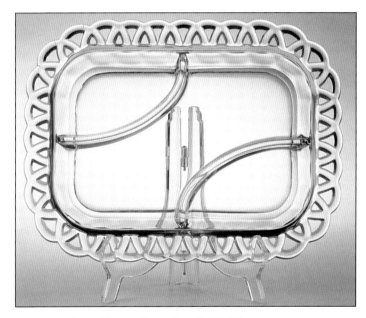

7800: 11 1/2" or 12" Relish Dish, Crystal, $22-25

7800: 11 1/2" or 12" Relish Dish (oblong)
Crystal
PL 38-42, SN 39-63, PH 43-50, SN 54-55

780/6: 11 1/2" Relish Dish (oblong) (Intaglio Vegetables)
Crystal
Cat/PL 40s-50s

1950/215: Partitioned Relish Tray
Milk Glass, Doeskin
PL 54-55
Began production 1/1/55

7801C: 7 1/2" Compote, 4-Toed, Crimped, Imperial Green, $28-31

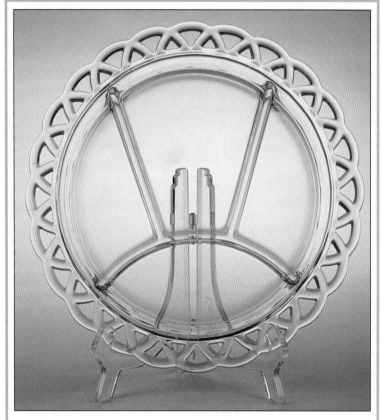

7801: 10 1/2" Hors d'oeuvres, Crystal, $22-25

7801: 10 1/2" Hors d'oeuvres (round)
Crystal
PL 38-42, PL 6/29/49, PH 43-50,
SN 54-55

7801C: 7 1/2" Compote, 4-Toed, Crimped
Crystal, Imperial Green, Blue, Topaz, Green
PL 38-42
Crystal
SN 39-63, Cat/PL 40s-50s
Other color: aftermarket silvery coating

7801C/cut 273
Crystal
PL 38-42

7801C(?)/cut V
Crystal
Undocumented

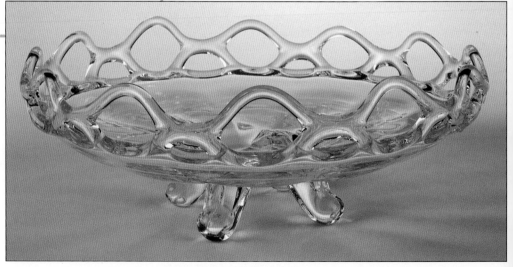

7801F: 7 1/2" Compote, 4-Toed, Shallow, Crystal, $28-31

7801F: 7 1/2" Compote, 4-Toed, Shallow
Crystal
PL 38-42, SN 39-63, Cat/PL 40s-50s, SN 54-55

7801F/cut 273
Crystal
PL 38-42

7801S: 6" Square Bon Bon, 4-Toed, Steigel Green, $28-31

7801S or 780S: 6" Square Bon Bon, 4-Toed
Crystal
Cat 36?-40?
Other colors: Steigel Green, Ritz Blue, Amber

7801S(?)/cut 273
Crystal
Undocumented

7801S(?)/cut II
Crystal
Undocumented

7801K: 5" Vase, 4-Toed, Amber, $28-31

7801K or 780K: 5" Vase, 4-Toed
Crystal
Cat 36?-40?
Other colors: Steigel Green, Ritz Blue, Amber

7801K(?)/cut 273
Crystal
Undocumented

7801W: 7 1/2" Comport, 4-Toed, Blue, $28-31

7801W or 780W: 7 1/2" Comport, 4-Toed
Crystal
Cat 36?-40?, Cat/PL 40s-50s, PL 6/29/49, PH 43-50, SN 54-55
Crystal, Blue, Topaz, Green
PL 38-42, SN 39-63

Other colors: Steigel Green, Ritz Blue, Amber, aftermarket silvery coating

7801W/cut 273
Crystal
PL 38-42

7801W(?)/cut I
Crystal
Undocumented

7801W(?)/cut VI
Crystal
Undocumented

7802: 10" Celery Dish, Crystal, $40-45

7802: 10" Celery Dish
Crystal
SN 39-63, PH 43-50, SN 54-55

7801Z: 4 1/2" Rose Bowl, 4-Toed, Ritz Blue, $35-38

7801Z or 780Z: 4 1/2" Rose Bowl, 4-Toed
Crystal
Cat 36?-40?
Other colors: Steigel Green, Ritz Blue, Amber

7801Z(?)/cut 273
Crystal
Undocumented

7802B: 6" Bowl, Belled Shape, Pearl, $18-21

7802B: 6" Bowl, Belled Shape
Crystal
PL 38-42, Cat/PL 40s-50s, SN 54-55
Other colors: Steigel Green, Ritz Blue, Amber, Pearl, Seafoam Blue, aftermarket silvery coating

7802B/cut 272: 6 1/2" Belled Nappy
Crystal
PL 38-42

7802B/cut 273
Crystal
PL 38-42

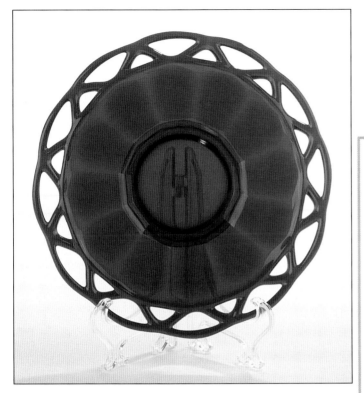

7802D: 7 1/2" Plate, Ritz Blue, $18-21

7802D: 7 1/2" Plate
Crystal
PL 38-42, SN 54-55
Other colors: Steigel Green, Ritz Blue, Amber, Pearl

7802D/cut 272
Crystal
PL 38-42

7802K: 3 1/2" Flower Bowl, Flashed Cranberry, $18-21

7802K: 3 1/2" Flower Bowl
Crystal
Cat/PL 40s-50s, SN 54-55
Other color: Flashed Cranberry

7802F: 6 1/2" Nappy, Amber, $14-16

7802F: 6 1/2" Nappy (Shallow)
Crystal
PL 38-42, SN 39-63, PL 6/29/49, SN
54-55

Other colors: Steigel Green, Ritz Blue,
Amber, Pearl, aftermarket silvery
coating

7802F/cut 272
Crystal
PL 38-42

7802N: 5" Flower Bowl, aftermarket
silvery coating, $22-25

7802N: 5" Flower Bowl
Crystal
SN 39-63, SN 54-55
Other colors: aftermarket silvery coating

1950/1723: 7 3/4" Basket, Milk Glass, $22-25

7802/0: 7 3/4" Basket
Crystal
SN 39-63, PH 43-50

1950/1723: 7 3/4" Basket
Milk Glass
Cat D-mid 50s, Cat E-late 50s, SN 57-58, Cat 57 Sup, PL 58, PL 61

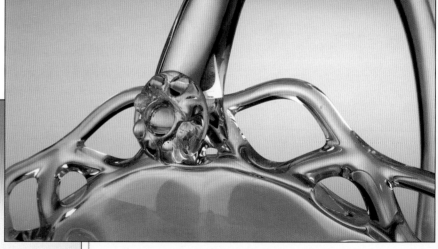

Detail of handle attachment on basket

7802/0: 7 3/4" Basket, Crystal, $50-55

7803K: 5" Vase, 4-Toed, Cut in Top, Amber, $22-25

7803K: 5" Vase, 4-Toed, Cut in Top
Crystal
PL 38-42, Cat/PL 40s-50s, SN 54-55
Other colors: Steigel Green, Ritz Blue, Amber

7803K(?)/cut 272
Crystal
Undocumented

7803B: 5" Vase, 4-Toed, Belled Top, Flashed Cranberry, $28-31

7803B: 5" Vase, 4-Toed, Belled Top (Violet Bowl)
Crystal
PL 38-42, SN 39-63, Cat/PL 40s-50s, PH 43-50, PL 6/29/49, SN 54-55
Other colors: Steigel Green, Ritz Blue, Amber, Seafoam Blue, Flashed Cranberry

7803B/cut 272: 5" Vase, 4-Toed, Belled Top
Crystal
PL 38-42

7803N: 5" Vase, 4-Toed, Steigel Green, $22-25

91

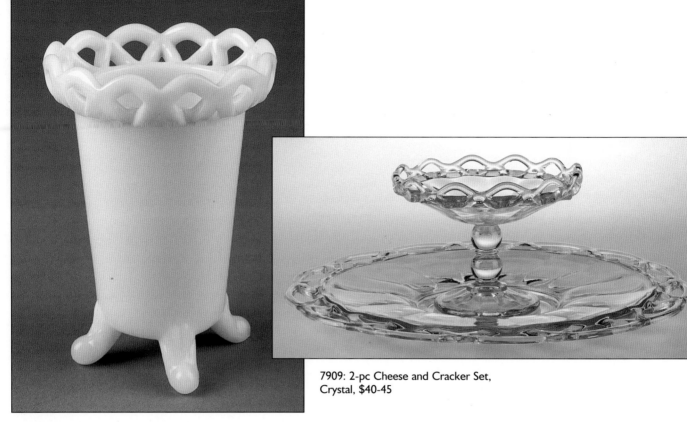

11/7803N (?): 5" Vase, 4-Toed, Milk Glass, $35-40

7803N: 5" Vase, 4-Toed (Base-star)
Crystal
Cat/PL 40s-50s
Other colors: Steigel Green, Ritz Blue, Amber

7803N: 5" Vase, 4-Toed (Base-clear)
Crystal
PL 38-42
Other colors: Pearl

7803N/cut 272: 5"
Vase, 4-Toed
Crystal
PL 38-42

11/7803N(?)
Milk Glass
Undocumented

7909: 2-pc Cheese and Cracker Set,
Crystal, $40-45

7804F: 6 1/2" Ftd. Jelly (in Cheese and Cracker Set)
Crystal
SN 39-63, PL 6/29/49, SN 54-55
Other colors: aftermarket silvery coating

7909: 2-pc Cheese and Cracker Set – 12" Plate (7808D), 6 1/2" Ftd Jelly (7804F)
Crystal
SN 39-63, PH 43-50, PL 6/29/49, SN 54-55

7804B: 5 1/2" Ftd. Jelly, Crystal, $18-20

7804B: 5 1/2" Ftd. Jelly
Crystal
SN 39-63, PH 43-50
Other colors: Flashed Cranberry

7805B: 5 1/2" Low Compote, Flashed Cranberry, $25-28

7809: 3-pc Buffet Set, Crystal, $60-65

7805B: 5 1/2" Low Comporte (in Buffet Set)
Crystal
SN 39-63, SN 54-55
Other colors: Flashed Cranberry, aftermarket silvery coating

7805B(?)/cut VII: 5 1/2" Low Comporte
Crystal
Undocumented

7809: 3-pc Buffet Set – 14" Plate (7809D), 5 1/2" Low Comporte (7805B), Ladle (615)
Crystal
SN 39-63, PH 43-50, PL 6/29/49, SN 54-55

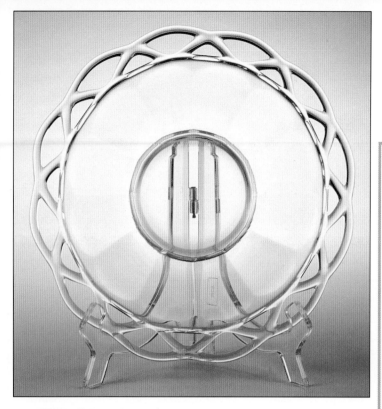

7805D: 8" Plate, Crystal, $14-16

7805D: 8" Plate
Crystal
SN 39-63, PH 43-50, PL 6/29/49, SN 54-55

7805D: 7 1/2" Plate (not paneled) (*Not pictured*)
Crystal
Cat 36?-40?

7805K(?)/cut II, 3" Sweet Pea, Crystal, $18-21

7805K: 3" Sweet Pea (not paneled)
Crystal
Cat 36?-40?

7805K(?)/cut II
Crystal
Undocumented

7805F(?)/cut III, 6 1/2" Nappy, Crystal, $18-21

7805F(?)/cut III
Crystal
Undocumented

7805F: 6 1/2" Nappy (Shallow) (not paneled)
Crystal
Cat 36?-40?

7805S(?)/cut 272, 6" Square Nappy, Crystal, $18-21

7805S: 6" Square Nappy (not paneled)
Crystal
Cat 36?-40?

7805S(?)/cut 272
Crystal
Undocumented

7805S(?)/cut III
Crystal
Undocumented

7806B(?)/cut IV, Crystal, $25-28

7806B: 7 3/4" Bowl, Belled
Crystal
PL 38-42, SN 54-55

7806B(?)/cut IV
Crystal
Undocumented

7806/3B: 7 3/4" Bowl, Belled (Intaglio Apple and Pear)
Crystal
PL 38-42

7805W: 5 1/2" Deep Bowl, Crystal, $14-16

7805W. 5 1/2" Deep Bowl (not paneled)
Crystal
Cat 36?-40?
Other Color: Ritz Blue

7805W(?)/cut III
Crystal
Undocumented

7806C(?): 7 3/4" Bowl, Crimped
Crystal
Undocumented

7806C(?)/cut IV
Crystal
Undocumented

7806/3C: 7 3/4" Bowl, Crimped (Intaglio Apple and Pear)
Crystal
Cat/PL 40s-50s, PL 41
Other color: Topaz

7806/3C: 3-pc Console - 7 3/4" Bowl, Crimped (Intaglio Apple and Pear), 4 1/2" Candleholders (780)
Crystal
PL 41

7806/3C: 7 3/4" Bowl, Crimped, Topaz, $25-28

11/7806D (?): 9 1/2" Plate, Milk Glass, $18-20

7806D: 9 1/2" Plate
Crystal
Cat/PL 40s-50s, PH 43-50, PL 6/29/49, SN 54-55
Crystal, Blue, Topaz, Green
PL 38-42

7806D/cut 273
Crystal
PL 38-42

7806/3D: 9 1/2" Plate (Intaglio Apple and Pear)
Crystal
PL 38-42, Cat/PL 40s-50s, PL 41

11/7806D(?): 9 1/2" Plate
Milk Glass
Undocumented

7806(?)/3E: 8 1/2" Basket Bowl, Blue, $35-40

7806(?)/3E: 8 1/2" Basket Bowl (Intaglio Apple and Pear)
Crystal
Undocumented
Other color: Blue

7806F: 8" Walnut Bowl, Crystal, $18-20

7806F: 8" Walnut Bowl
Crystal
SN 39-63, PH 43-50, PL 6/29/49, SN 54-55
Crystal, Blue, Topaz, Green
PL 38-42
Other color: aftermarket silvery coating

7806F(?)/cut I
Crystal
Undocumented

7806F(?)/cut IV
Crystal
Undocumented

7806/3F: 8" Bowl (Intaglio Apple and Pear)
Crystal
PL 38-42, Cat/PL 40s-50s, PL 41

7806(?)/3F: 8" Bowl (Intaglio Apple and Pear) (on silver stand)
Crystal
Undocumented

7806K: 4 1/2" Flower Bowl (*Not pictured; compare 7802K above*)
Crystal
PL 38-42, SN 54-55

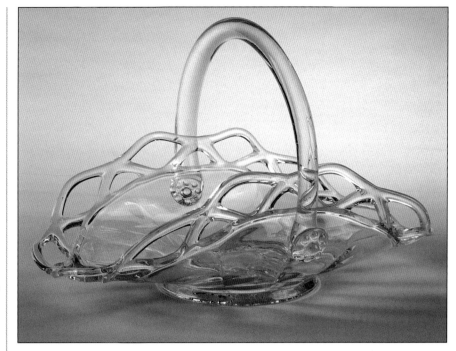

7806/0/3F: 9 1/2" Basket, Crystal, $70-75

7806/0/3F: 9 1/2" Basket
Crystal
SN 39-63, PH 43-50

7806/0/3F: 9 1/2" Basket (Intaglio Apple and Pear)
Crystal
PL 38-42, PL 41, PH 43-50

7806N: 5 1/2" Flower Bowl, Crystal, $22-25

7806N: 5 1/2" Flower Bowl
Crystal
SN 54-55

7806/3X: 8" Bowl (Intaglio Apple and Pear) (*Not pictured*)
Crystal, Blue, Topaz, Green
PL 38-42

7808B: 8" Trumpet
Bouquet, Crystal, $60-65

7808B: 8" Trumpet Bouquet
Crystal
SN 39-63, PH 43-50, PL 6/29/49, SN 54-55

7808B: 10" Bowl, Belled (*Not pictured; compare 7809B below*)
Crystal
SN 54-55

7808D/cut 269: 3-pc Console - 10" Bowl (7808B/cut 269), 4 1/2"
Candleholders (780)
Crystal
PL 41

7808/3B: 10" Bowl, Belled (Intaglio Apple and Pear)
Crystal
PH 33-44, PL 38-42, SN 45-46
Discontinued 1/1/46

7808/3B: 3-pc Console - 10" Bowl (7808B) (Intaglio Apple and Pear), 4
1/2" Candleholders (780)
Crystal
SN 45-46
Discontinued 1/1/46

7808C: 10" Crimped Bowl, Plain Bottom
Crystal
Cat/PL 40s-50s, PL 41

7808C: 3-pc Console -10" Crimped Bowl, Plain Bottom (7808C),
4 1/2" Candleholders (780)
Crystal
Cat/PL 40s-50s, PL 41

78C: 3-pc Console -10" Crimped Bowl, Plain Bottom (7808C),
Candleholders Crimped (78C)
Crystal
Cat/PL 40s-50s, PL 41

7808/9C: 4-pc Salad Set - 10" Crimped Bowl (7808C), 12" or 13"
Plate (7808D), Fork and Spoon (701)
Crystal
SN 54-55

7808C/cut 120: 10" Crimped Bowl, Plain Bottom
Crystal
PL 41

78C/cut 120: 3-pc Console -10" Crimped Bowl, Plain Bottom
(7808C/cut 120), Candleholders Crimped (78C)
Crystal
PL 41

7808/3C: 10" Bowl, Crimped (Intaglio Apple and Pear)
Crystal
SN 39-63, Cat/PL 40s-50s, PH 43-50

78/3C or 7808/3C/78C: 3-pc Console - 10" Bowl, Crimped
(Intaglio Apple and Pear) (7808/3C), Candleholders Crimped
(78C)
Crystal
PL 38-42, PL 41

7808/3C: 3-pc Console - 10" Bowl, Crimped (Intaglio Apple and
Pear) (7808/3C), 4 1/2" Candleholders (780)
Crystal
Cat/PL 40s-50s

7808/3C: 10" Bowl, Crimped, Crystal, $28-31

7808/3C/78C: 3-pc Console, Crystal, $55-60

7808D: 12" Plate, Crystal, $22-25

11/7808D(?): 12" Plate, Milk Glass, $22-25

7808D: 12" or 13" Plate
Crystal
SN 39-63, PL 6/29/49, SN 54-55

7808/3D: 12" Plate (Intaglio Apple and Pear)
Crystal
PL 38-42, Cat/PL 40s-50s, SN 45-46
Discontinued 1/1/46

11/7808D(?): 12" Plate
Milk Glass
Undocumented

7808F: 3-pc Console, Crystal, $50-55

78KF: 3-pc Console, Crystal, $60-65

7808F: 11" Bowl, Crystal, $28-31

11/7808F(?): 11" Bowl, Milk
Glass, $22-25

7808F(?): 11" Bowl, Purple Slag, $235-245

7808F: 11" Bowl, Shallow, Plain Bottom
Crystal
PL 38-42, SN 39-63, Cat/PL 40s-50s, PL 41, PH 43-59, PL 6/29/49, SN 54-55

7808F: 3-pc Console - 11" Bowl, Shallow, Plain Bottom (7808F), 4 1/2" Candleholders (780)
Crystal
PL 38-42, Cat/PL 40s-50s, PL 6/29/49, PH (no date)

78KF: 3-pc Console - 11" Bowl, Shallow, Plain Bottom (7808F), Candleholders (78K)
Crystal
Cat/PL 40s-50s, PL 41

7808F/cut 120: 11" Bowl, Shallow, Plain Bottom
Crystal
PL 41

78KF/cut 120: 3-pc Console - 11" Bowl, Shallow, Plain Bottom (7808F/cut 120), Candleholders (78K)
Crystal
PL 41

7808F/cut 269: 11" Bowl, Shallow, Plain Bottom
Crystal
PL 41

7808F/cut 269: 3-pc Console - 11" Bowl, Shallow, Plain Bottom (7808F/cut 120), 4 1/2" Candleholders (780)
Crystal
PL 41

7808/3F: 11" Bowl, Shallow, Plain Bottom (Intaglio Apple and Pear)
Crystal
PL 38-42, Cat/PL 40s-50s, PL 41

7808/3F: 3-pc Console - 11" Bowl, Shallow, Plain Bottom (Intaglio Apple and Pear) (7808/3F), 4 1/2" Candleholders (780)
Crystal
PL 38-42, PL 41

78/3KF: 3-pc Console - 11" Bowl, Shallow, Plain Bottom (Intaglio Apple and Pear) (7808/3F), Candleholders (78K)
Crystal
PL 41

11/7808F(?): 11" Bowl, Shallow, Plain Bottom
Milk Glass
Undocumented

7808F(?)
Purple Slag
Undocumented

7808K: 7" Narcissus Bowl, Crystal, $40-45

7808K: 7" Narcissus Bowl
Crystal
SN 39-63, PL 41, PH 43-50, PL 6/29/49, SN 54-55

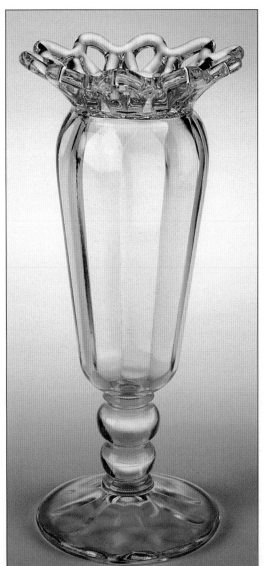

7808/0: 12 1/2" Basket, Crystal, $140-150

7808/0: 12 1/2" or 13" Basket
Crystal
PL 38-42, SN 39-63, PH 43-50

7808/0/3F: 12 1/2" or 13" Basket (Intaglio Apple and Pear)
Crystal
PH 43-50

1950/1725: 12 1/2" or 13" Basket
Milk Glass
Cat D-mid 50s, Cat E-late 50s, SN 57-58, PL 58, PL 61

7808K: 8" Bud Bouquet, Crystal, $60-65

7808K: 8" Bud Bouquet
Crystal
SN 39-63, PH 43-50, PL 6/29/49, SN 54-55

7808N: 7" Flower Bowl (*Not pictured; compare 7806N above*)
Crystal
Cat/PL 40s-50s, PL 41, SN 54-55

7808/9: 4-pc Salad Set, Crystal, $70-75

7809B: 10 1/2" or 11" Salad Bowl
Crystal
SN 39-63, PH 43-50, PL 6/29/49, SN 54-55

7808/9: 4-pc Salad Set - 10 1/2" or 11" Salad Bowl (7809B), 12" or 13" Plate (7808D), Fork and Spoon (701)
Crystal
SN 39-63, PH 43-50, PL 6/29/49, SN 54-55

701: Fork and Spoon (in Salad Set)
Crystal
PL 38-42, PH 38, SN 39-63, PL 6/29/49

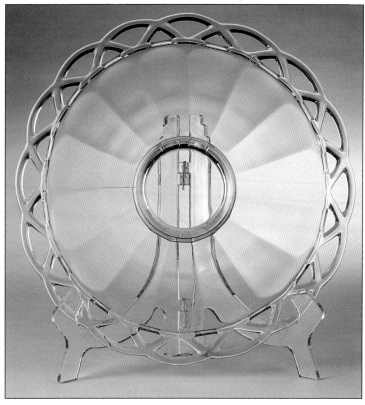

7809D: 14" Plate, Crystal, $28-31

7809D: 14" Plate
Crystal
SN 39-63, PH 43-50, PL 6/29/49, SN 54-55

7809C: 12" Crimped Bowl, Crystal, $35-40

7809C: 12" Crimped Bowl
Crystal
SN 39-63, PH 43-50, PL 6/29/49, SN 54-55

78010B: Punch Bowl; both 780 Punch Cups; 703 and 780/91 Punch Ladles; Crystal; 14-pc. Punch Bowl Set price would be $115-125

78010 or 780: 14- or 15-pc Punch Bowl Set - Punch Bowl (78010B), 12" or 13" Plate (7808D) (15-pc only), Punch Cups (780), Punch Ladle (703)
Crystal
PL 38-42, SN 39-63, PH 43-50, PL 6/29/49, SN 54-55, Cat 62

78010B: Punch Bowl
Crystal
PL 6/29/49, SN 54-55, PH 64

780: Punch Cup – old style
Crystal
PL 38-42, PH (no date)

780 (or 78010): Punch Cup – new style
Crystal
PL 38-42, PH 43-50, PL 6/29/49, SN 54-55

780/91: Punch Ladle
Crystal
Cat 66A

703 (or 78010): Punch Ladle
Crystal
PL 38-42, PL 6/29/49, SN 54-55, PH (no date)

780: 14-Punch Set - Punch Bowl (78010B), Punch Cups (780), Punch Ladle (780/91)
Purple Slag with Crystal Ladle
Cat 62 Sup One, PH 64
Began production 7/1/62; discontinued 12/31/63

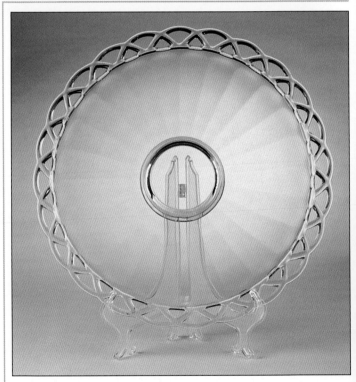

78010D: 17" Plate, Crystal, $70-75

78010D: 17" Plate
Crystal
SN 39-63, PH 43-50, PL 6/29/49, SN 54-55

Chapter 6

Additions to Lace Edge Pieces

Collectors may find Lace Edge pieces with metal bases, handles, or stands, with decals or painted decoration, and with a metallic coating. If the Imperial documents show these items for sale, Imperial produced the pieces and shipped them with the additions already attached or applied. Extant records list orders for plain pieces by several companies in the business of lighting, metals, or glass cutting. It can reasonably be assumed these companies added their own touches before passing the items along to consumers. Without complete records, collectors cannot discover the origin of every addition.

Factory Attachments – Stands, Handles, Bases

The Salesman's Notebook from 1957-1958 illustrates the 1950/B207C 7 1/2" Crimped Bowl, a Milk Glass bowl on a brass base. This is an example of a piece which had the base attached at the factory. Imperial would have purchased the brass piece from another company. The brass was put in place while the glass was still warm, ensuring the permanence of the pairing. The same would be true for the 1950/B790 Sugar and Cream Set from the same Notebook.

Several pieces of Lace Edge have metal additions that are removable. Shown in Imperial documents for sale, these pieces come with metal fitted but not permanently attached. Imperial would have purchased the metal and shipped it to customers with the glass. Here is a list of Lace Edge pieces sold from the Imperial factory with removable metal parts:

1950/749F	7" Comporte/Brass Handle Server
745	Ivy Ball with Chain
7497K	6 1/2" Rose Bowl and Holder
7497R	6 1/2" Flower Bowl and Holder
7498K	7 1/2" Rose Bowl and Holder
7498R	7 1/2" Flower Bowl and Holder
7432/86	Tid Bit Set – 12" and 9 1/2" Plates
7497/9	Tid Bit Set – 14" and 11" Plates
7498/97	Tid Bit Set – 12" and 11" Plates
74910/6	Tid Bit Set – 10" and 8" Plates

Ivy ball chains and metal holders for rose or flower bowls are seldom found because the metal has rusted over the years. Any item on this list in original condition is very rare. Refer to Chapter 5 Mould Number List and Pictures to see pieces with metal added.

Processing by Other Companies – Stands, Decals, Handles, Bases, Coating

The Price Lists from 1938-1942 and the Salesman's Notebook from 1939-1963 include order sheets for dozens of companies. Most of these orders were placed in the 1940s. Records from other years are not known to exist any longer. The exact timing is not as important as knowing what kinds of companies were buying Imperial glass. Retailers and distributors make up the majority of the companies that ordered Lace Edge. Four lighting companies, a glass cutting company, and four metal companies also bought Lace Edge.

The four lighting companies were Centre Lighting Fixture Mfg. Co., Imperial Lighting Products Company, Premier Lamp Company, and Quality Lamp and Shade Company, Incorporated. Included in their orders were these pieces:

7498B	10" Bowl, Belled
7498F	11" Bowl, Shallow
7499F	13" Fruit Bowl
7499/4F	13" Fruit Bowl (Intaglio Grapes)
7499V	13" Torte Plate
78K/cut 272	Candleholder
7801F/cut 273	7 1/2" Compote, 4-Toed, Shallow
7803N	5" Vase, 4-Toed
7808/3F	11" Bowl, Shallow (Intaglio Apple/Pear)

Imperial Glass drilled holes for wiring or hanging of lights if the lighting companies ordered the holes done. For example, the 7803N 5" Vase, 4-Toed would have a hole drilled in the bottom to allow the wires to run to an outlet from a center tube that supported the light bulb and shade. A large bowl would have been drilled to allow fastening to the electrical fixture on the ceiling. The collector who finds a lamp or light fixture made from a piece of Lace Edge has a rare item indeed.

The Marion Glass Manufacturing Company specialized in cutting designs on glass. This company ordered ten types of plates, bowls, and compotes in the 780 line. As noted above for metal additions, if an Imperial document showed a Lace Edge piece with a particular cut, the piece was shipped by Imperial with that cut. An Imperial subsidiary named Crown Glass Manufacturing Company did the cutting. If a collector finds a 780 piece with a cut not documented as Imperial or Crown, it could have come from Marion Glass.

Globe Silver Company, Incorporated placed orders for these five items:

7436/5B	7 3/4" Bowl (Intaglio Roses)
7436/5D	9 1/2" Plate (Intaglio Roses)
7497B	9" Bowl (Belled)
7806/3B	7 3/4" Bowl, Belled (Intaglio Apple/Pear)
7806/3D	9 1/2" Plate (Intaglio Apple/ Pear)

The picture is presented as an illustration of what might have been created by Globe from the intaglio pieces it bought. The only marking on the piece indicates it is silver electroplated on a copper base. No extant order states that Globe Silver bought the 7806/3F from Imperial, and no extant Imperial document states that Imperial added the base before shipment.

The Kromex Corporation orders included these pieces:

169	5" Ladle
615	5" Ladle, rounded
749	Sugar and Creamer Set
749	9 ounce Tumbler

The 749 Tumbler and the 615 Ladle fit together with a chrome lid. The chrome lid in the picture has no markings, so it may have been made by another company specializing in chrome besides Kromex. Whoever created this combination, the result was a lovely jelly jar complete with serving spoon.

7806/3F: 8" Bowl (Intaglio Apple and Pear) on Silver Stand, Crystal

749: 9 ounce Tumbler, 615 Ladle, and Chrome Lid, Crystal

La Belle Silver Company ordered the 7498D 12" Plate, but it is not known whether La Belle produced the handle for this 12" Plate. What is known is that the plate was found for sale with the removable metal handle attached. Using such a handle to carry the weight of a plate full of food would seem to be a guarantee of disaster, but as a display or centerpiece, the handle adds a striking plus.

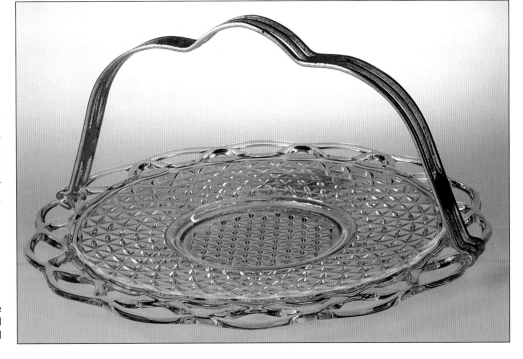

7498D: 12" Plate with Metal Handle, Crystal

The last company mentioned as a metal company was Silvalyte. This company bought glass from Imperial, coated it with a coating that makes the piece look like mercury or silver, and sold it with their Silvalyte sticker on each piece. The list of Lace Edge ordered by Silvalyte included these items:

78C	Candleholder Crimped
78K	Candleholder
7801C	7 1/2" Compote, 4-Toed, Crimped
7801W	7 1/2" Compote, 4-Toed
7802B	6" Bowl, Belled Shape
7802F	6 1/2" Nappy (Shallow)
7802N	5" Flower Bowl

7804F	6 1/2" Footed Jelly
7805B	5 1/2" Low Comporte
7806F	8" Walnut Bowl
7808F	11" Bowl, Shallow

Silvalyte also ordered the 400/152 Chimney, which fits the 78C Candleholder.

Aftermarket Changes

Collectors may find Lace Edge pieces that have been altered by companies other than those mentioned or by individuals. It is easier to tell with some pieces than with others exactly who made the alterations to the originals.

78K: Candleholders, Silvalyte Coating

7801C: 7 1/2" Compote, 4-Toed, Crimped, Silvalyte Coating

7801W: 7 1/2" Comport, 4-Toed,
Silvalyte Coating

7802B: 6" Bowl, Belled
Shape, Silvalyte Coating

7802N: 5" Flower Bowl,
Silvalyte Coating

7804F: 6 1/2" Ftd. Jelly, Silvalyte Coating

7805B: 5 1/2" Low Comporte, Silvalyte Coating

7806F: 8" Bowl, Silvalyte Coating

Silvalyte sticker

For example, occasionally one comes across a plate with a decal, such as the two shown. I have found the anniversary decal on more than one 7808D 12" Plate, which indicates the decal may have been applied by a company rather than an individual. Imperial did not affix decals to plates.

7805D: 8" Plate with Decal, Crystal

7808D: 12" Plate with Decal, Crystal

This Crystal nappy on a chrome stand offers the following information on the base of the stand: "Diana Chrome, Farber and Shlevin, Inc., Brooklyn, NY." It is reasonable to conclude that Farber, a metal company, bought the 7455F 6 3/4" Nappy from Imperial and added the stand. Imperial may have drilled the hole before shipment

The stand in which this 7455F Nappy sits was clearly made for this purpose. The fit is tight, but the nappy can be removed. The type of stand is reminiscent of those used for some Cape Cod pieces and may have been purchased by Imperial for this particular use. This combination does not appear in an extant Imperial publication, so one can only surmise whether Imperial sold this nappy and stand as a pair. If not Imperial, then another company specially ordered this nappy in Satin and paired it with the stand. This is the only piece of Lace Edge I have seen in Satin, and I have found none in catalogs.

7455F: 6 3/4" Nappy on
Chrome Stand, Crystal

This Lace Edge item is not found in an Imperial catalog, although the bowl is definitely a 7455F 6 3/4" Nappy. I have seen this unmarked statue used as a base for an Imperial Cape Cod bowl also.

7455F: 6 3/4" Nappy in Metal Basket, Satin

7455F: 6 3/4" Nappy on
Cupid Stand, Ruby

Although the aluminum handle fits across this Blue 7806/3E 8 1/2" Basket Bowl (Intaglio Apple/Pear), using the handle means taking a chance with breaking the loops. The glass itself does not appear in any known Imperial catalog, so the number is a theoretical one. However, the size and design match the other 7806 pieces. It is possible that a metal company ordered the piece made to their specifications.

7806(?)/3E: 8 1/2" Basket Bowl (Intaglio Apple and Pear) with Metal Handle, Blue

There is always the possibility of the collector seeing the absurd passed off as a real find. This illustration shows a Seafoam Blue 749 Saucer with a chrome handle as they were found at an antique mall. Is the collector to believe the cup is missing from this vignette? Or is she not supposed to notice this is a saucer and not a plate? No Imperial catalog includes this particular combination.

749: Saucer with Metal Handle, Seafoam Blue

Imperial did produce hand-painted pieces of glass, but no painted Lace Edge pieces are listed for sale in Imperial documents. After painting at the factory, the glass was heated again to bake the paint on securely. With aftermarket painting, colors are often found in poor condition and can usually be removed without much effort. All the pieces pictured here were painted after leaving the factory. The gold on the Nappy's roses is flaking off, and the gold around the rim of the Crimped Bowl is wearing away. Care has been taken to preserve the floral arrangements depicted on the 6" Bowl, which may also be the newest of the pieces. The flowers look freshly done, and the artist's signature is intact.

1950/207C: 7 1/2" Crimped Bowl with Painted Flowers, Milk Glass

1950/745F: 6" Shallow Bowl with Painted Flowers, Milk Glass

Detail of Painted Flowers

743B: 5 1/2" Vase, 4-Toed, Ritz
Blue with Painted Toes

7436/5F: 8" Nappy with Painted Intaglio
Roses, Crystal

7498/4D: 12" Plate with Painted Intaglio Grapes, Crystal

Chapter 7

Related Pieces by Imperial

Similarities and differences from main 743, 745, 749, and 780 Lace Edge pieces appear obvious when examining other glass patterns produced by Imperial. Edges may bear a resemblance to Lace Edge. Mould numbers are dissimilar but ending letters may mean the same as with Lace Edge. Some other types of pieces also have the name Lace Edge.

Cut Edge

Eleven pieces that resembled Lace Edge but with cut edges instead of gracefully crossed loops appeared in Catalog E in the late 1950s. The Salesman's Notebook from 1957-58 and Price Lists from 1958 and 1961 show the same pieces as available. At that time, Milk Glass was very popular, and these pieces were all Milk Glass. Myrna and Bob Garrison's *Milk Glass: The Imperial Glass Corporation* calls them "Lace Edge Cut." Imperial used numbers but not a pattern name for these items. The eleven pieces included the following:

1950/360D	12" Footed Cake Stand
1950/360E	12" Footed Banana Boat
1950/360F	10" Footed Fruit Bowl
1950/361F	10" Bowl (Shallow)
1950/362F	8" Bowl (Shallow)
1950/363F	6" Bowl (Shallow)
1950/364F	7" Compote
1950/365B	7" 4-Toed Compote
1950/366C	6" Candleholder (Crimped)
1950/367	7 3/4" Basket
1950/368	12 1/2" Basket

Cut 1950/360F: 10" Fruit Bowl, Milk Glass

Cut 1950/360D: 12" Footed Cake
Stand, Milk Glass

The baskets are quite rare, but the other pieces are sometimes seen in antique malls. Note that the mould numbers are in numerical order and bear no resemblance to the numbers for the corresponding Lace Edge pieces. However, the letters at the ends of the mould numbers are used in a manner consistent with the letters on Lace Edge mould numbers.

Cut 1950/362F: 8" Bowl (Shallow), Milk Glass

Cut 1950/365B: 7" 4-Toed Compote, Milk Glass

Cut 1950/363F: 6" Bowl
(Shallow), Milk Glass

Cut 1950/366C: 6" Candleholder (Crimped), Milk Glass

Imperial made a Purple Slag 363F 6" Bowl (Shallow) in glossy only. This piece was first available on January 1, 1961, and discontinued December 31, 1968.

Cut 363F: 6" Bowl (Shallow), Purple Slag (glossy)

Star Holly, Leaf, and Open Leaf

The Sears, Roebuck and Company catalog for Fall and Winter 1950 included a variation of what appear to be many of the optic or paneled Crocheted Crystal pieces, but with a different edging. The Crystal punch bowl and cups, several sizes of plates and bowls, and the mayonnaise set were similar in size and shape to those Crocheted Crystal pieces offered earlier. Other pieces in this catalog had new bases or shapes.

The edge was an overlapping leaf pattern with no openings between the leaves. Sears carried twenty-three items or sets and called the pattern Leaf Fantasy. The catalog makes no reference to Imperial by name but does mention the "Outstanding designer" who made this pattern exclusively for Sears. The text goes on to refer to the "Famous manufacturer" as "the finest glassware company we knew."

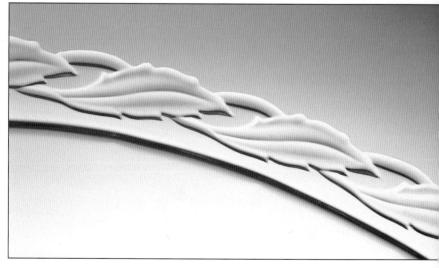

Leaf Fantasy Detail

Leaf Fantasy Cake Stand, Crystal

Leaf Fantasy Bowl, Crystal

With a large star added in the center of the pieces, Imperial called this crystal pattern Star Holly and marketed it to other customers. Imperial went on to make similar pieces in Milk Glass but did not use a pattern name. To help people refer to these pieces, the Garrisons call this version "Leaf" in their *Milk Glass: The Imperial Glass Corporation*. With a change to the edging that included a space between leaves, Imperial created another pattern. The Garrisons called this Milk Glass version "Leaf Open."

Imperial later sold both the closed and open leaf pieces in other colors. The Ruby Slag dates to the mid-1970s. Imperial did not call any Leaf or Leaf Open pieces by the name Lace Edge with the following exception. Four Leaf Open items appeared in Salesman's Notebooks for 1955 and 1957-1958, as well as the 1961 Price List:

1950/785	Candy Box and Cover, Lace Edge
1950/786	6 1/2" Bowl, Lace Edge
1950/815	9" Candy Bowl and Cover, Lace Edge
1950/816	9" Bowl, Lace Edge

Open Border and Other Open Edges

Records show that Imperial produced a number of patterns that had some kind of open edge. Often Imperial identified the pieces without a pattern name at all, just the mould number. Here are some examples of patterns not called Lace Edge, even though the openness of the edging might have invited that name.

Leaf 1950/700: 9 oz. Goblet, Milk Glass

Leaf 759: Butter Dish and Cover, Ruby Slag

Leaf 1950/710D: 10 1/2" Plate, Milk Glass

Leaf 1950/767X: 11" Footed Fruit Bowl, Milk Glass

Leaf Open 1950/818:
3-pc Mayonnaise Set,
Milk Glass

Leaf Open 1950/840: 11" Candle Float Bowl, Milk Glass

In the mid-1950s Imperial made several pieces with an open edging similar to the 749 crow's foot loop but with the paneled or optic sides and a variety of bases. Imperial dubbed this pattern Open Border, although not all pieces of this type were called by that name in the company's catalogs and price lists.

Open Border 1950/5D: 8" Salad
or Wall Plate, Milk Glass

Open Border 1950/203D: 10"
Cake Stand, Milk Glass

Open Border 1950/203F: 8 1/4" Fruit Bowl, Milk Glass

Open Border 1950/717: 10" Wall Plate Fruit, Milk Glass

This 159 7 1/4" Atterbury Bowl is in Antique Blue. Such pieces were not called Lace Edge but Open Edge. This bowl appeared in the 1966 Catalog. Similar bowls were the bases for animal lids, and the same open edging graced rectangular 465 bowls.

Open Edge 7 1/4" Atterbury Bowl, Antique Blue

Imperial documents did not refer to the open edge on this piece as Lace Edge or any name mentioned above. Loops on the edge of this 1950/304 Spoonholder Sugar and Lid do not cross over to match the Lace Edge motif. There is a similar Spoonholder Creamer. The set appeared in other colors up until the 1975-1976 Catalog, but the numbers were completely different. The Sugar was 51549, the Creamer 51546, and the Set 51545.

Three heart-shaped dishes with a looped edge appeared in several catalogs on pages showing Lace Edge pieces. The 1950/271 (5" Heart), 1950/272 (6" Heart), and 1950/273 (7" Heart) were in Catalog F-1960, Salesman's Notebook dated 1957-58, Price Lists from 1959 and 1961, and Photos 1948-1964. The set of all three (1950/750) also can be found in the same Salesman's Notebook and Photos. These pieces were available in Milk Glass and Doeskin.

1950/304: Spoon Holder Sugar, Milk Glass

Lace Edge 1950/271: 5" Heart, 1950/272: 6" Heart, and 1950/273: 7" Heart, Milk Glass

Other Lace Edge

Not all Imperial catalogs, price lists, or salesman's notebooks referred to every 743, 745, 749, or 780 piece as Lace Edge each time such an item appeared. The mould numbers told the tale instead. On the other hand, documents from the mid-1950s and again 1969 refer to a few pieces as Lace Edge, although the numbers do not follow the usual patterns and the edges are not the same as the other pieces.

Lace Edge 1950/272: 6" Heart, Milk Glass and Doeskin

Lace Edge 1950/750 Set of Three Hearts, Milk Glass

The 464 bowl shown on page 139 is called Lace Edge on the 1969 Price list. The loops making up the edge do not cross each other but are bisected instead. This bowl was available in several colors over the years of production but was not always called Lace Edge.

Here is a chart depicting which extant Imperial documents use the pattern name Lace Edge and which documents refer to Lace Edge pieces only by mould number. Documents not including any Lace Edge or related pieces are not shown on this list. Note these abbreviations: Cat – Catalog; PL – Price List; SN – Salesman's Notebook; and Sup – Supplement.

Records	Names Used
Cat 1936?-40?	Pages labeled Laced Edge – but some pieces on same page not Lace Edge
PL- 1938-42	Lace Edge used on some pages for some items
SN 1939-63	Sears items called Crocheted Crystal; Lace Edge name not used
Photos 1930s-70s	Occasional use of name – pages not all dated
SN 1937-65	Name not used
Cat/PL 1942-53	By color; name not used
SN 1945-46	Called Lace Edge (not used on cancellation list 1-46)
PL 9-4-46	Not called Lace Edge
Cat/PL 1940s-50s	Not called Lace Edge on Milk Glass or intaglio pages; Laced Edge on rest
Cat Late 40's	Called Laced Edge
PL 6-29-49	Called Laced Edge
Cat 1950s - 1960s	Name not used
Cat B – 1952	Not called Lace Edge on Milk Glass pages

Records	Names Used
Cat C – 1953	Not called Lace Edge on Milk Glass pages, except for some pieces
SN 1953-55	By color; name used on some Milk Glass, some others, and some Leaf Open
Cat D – mid 50s	Not called Lace Edge on Milk Glass pages, except for 1 piece (749B)
Cat E – late 50s	Not called Lace Edge on Milk Glass pages, except for 3 pieces (78C, 749B&F)
SN 1955-68	By color; name used on some, including Belmont
Cat 57 Sup	Not called Lace Edge on Milk Glass pages, except 1950/749F; in Collectors Cupboard
SN 1957-58	By color; name used on some Milk Glass, some others, and some Leaf Open
PL 58	Lace Edge on some (except Milk Glass) and some Leaf Open
PL 59	By color but name used on some
Cat F – 1960	Not called Lace Edge on Milk Glass pages, except for 749F and hearts (1950/271-2-3)
PL 61	By color; name used on some Milk Glass, Hearts, and some Leaf Open
Cat 62	By color or item; name not used
Cat 62 Sup One	By color but name used on some
PL 63	By color; name not used
Cat 1964-65	By color; name not used
Cat 66	By color; name not used
Cat 66A	By color; name not used
SN 1967-68	By color; name not used
PL 68	By color; name not used
Cat 69	By color; name not used
Cat 69A	By color; name not used

Records	Names Used	Records	Names Used
PL 69	Not called Lace Edge, except deep bowl 464	PL 1973	By color; name not used
		PL 4/15/73	By color; name not used
Cat 71R; 71Sup	By color; name not used	Slag 1977	By color; name not used
PL 1972	By color; name not used		

Lace Edge 464 bowl, an amber shade

Chapter 8

Open Edge Pieces by Other Manufacturers

The collector who sees a glass piece labeled Open Lace Edge with no manufacturer's name or the wrong one can discern what is Imperial and what is not. Color, quality, shape, and size offer clues to help collectors who are looking to buy Imperial's Lace Edge. There are also differences in the seam where the lace joins the piece.

Imperial moulds are still used occasionally by other companies. In the 1990s Mosser Glass, Inc., used the 220 mould owned by Mirror Images to produce the cake stand, banana bowl, and the fruit bowl in jadeite, as well as the fruit bowl in vaseline for Rosso & Rosso Wholesale Glass. The collector should remember that Imperial did not use these colors for Lace Edge. The 78 mould has also been used recently to produce a beaded-stem compote in vaseline.

Co-Operative Flint Glass Company made numerous pieces in their Lace Edge pattern. Westmoreland Glass Company of Pennsylvania produced several types of glass with lacey edges. Many of these edges are quite intricate. A name often incorrectly assigned to Imperial's Lace Edge is Old Colony or Open Lace by Anchor Hocking.

1990s vaseline footed fruit bowl made by Mosser Glass for Rosso & Rosso from 220 mould owned by Mirror Images.

Jadeite footed fruit bowl made from 220 mould by Mosser for Rosso.

Jadeite cake stand made from 220 mould by Mosser for Rosso.

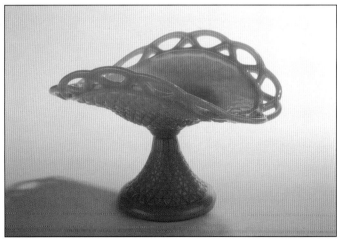

Jadeite banana bowl made from 220 mould by Mosser for Rosso.

Vaseline footed bowl made from 78 mould by unknown company.

Detail of Imperial Lace Edge. Note smooth line where lace meets bowl.

Footed fruit bowl in amber by
unknown manufacturer – not Imperial!

Detail of fruit bowl. Note how loops show
texture and continue into the bowl.

14" cake stand in green by same unknown manufacturer.

Banana boat in satin by same unknown manufacturer.

Banana boat in milk glass by same unknown manufacturer.

Purple compote by
Co-Operative Flint
about 1930.

Detail of purple compote. Note ends of loops rise
above the bowl surface. These bumps are found
on all the Co-Operative pieces and colors shown.

Light blue compote by Co-Operative Flint.

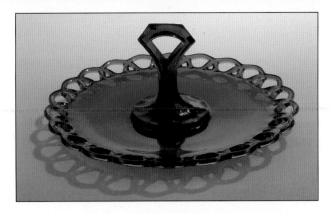

Handled tray by Co-Operative Flint in color very much like Imperial's Ultra Blue.

Black amethyst footed plate by Co-Operative Flint.

Blue footed plate with upright edge by Co-Operative Flint.

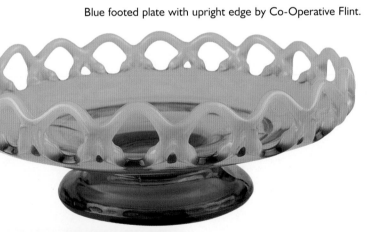

Flashed and crimped compote by Co-Operative Flint.

Milk glass footed plate by Co-Operative Flint.

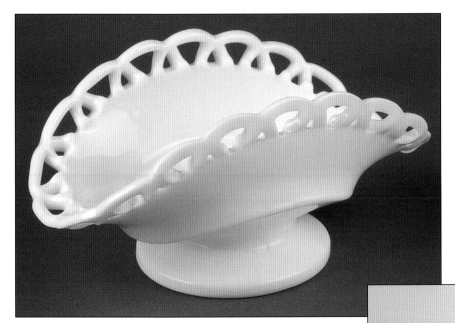

Milk glass basket bowl by Co-Operative Flint.

Crystal handled tray with upright edge by Co-Operative Flint.

Crystal flanged compote with cut by Co-Operative Flint.

Green Murano bowl by Duncan Miller.

Westmoreland bowl, one of many with lacey edges.

Milk glass Hazel Atlas bowl with closed edge.

Blue Hazel Atlas bowl with closed edge.

11" Fostoria (?) bowl with loops but no panels. Base is ground. Imperial did not make a bowl this size without panels.

Detail of Fostoria (?) bowl. Note wavy seam between lace and bowl. Imperial seams are smoother.

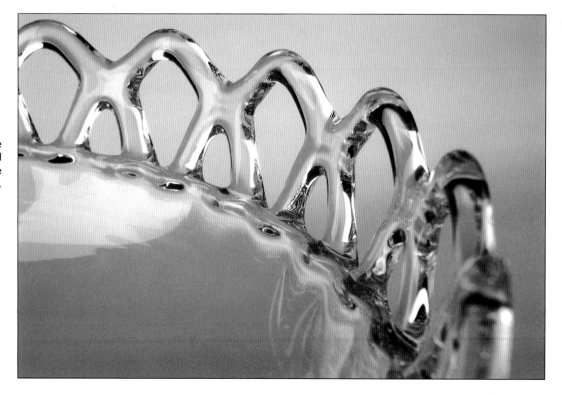

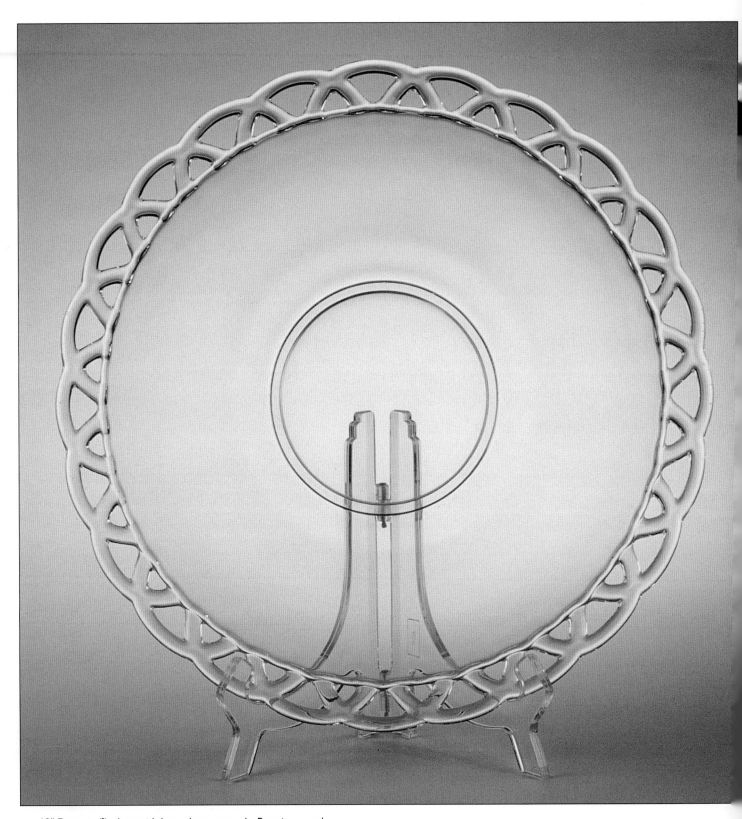

12" Fostoria (?) plate with loops but no panels. Base is ground.
Imperial did not make a plate this size without panels.

Anchor Hocking Old Colony bowl. Note loops do not cross to form triangles as they do on Imperial pieces.

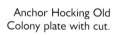

Anchor Hocking Old Colony plate with cut.

Amber flanged bowl by unknown manufacturer. Sides are not an Imperial pattern.

Blue flanged bowl by unknown manufacturer.

Crystal flanged bowl by unknown manufacturer.

Crystal bowl with loops and panels – but not Imperial! Piece has only been found in Canada but is by unknown manufacturer.

Detail of crystal bowl showing glass is much thicker than Imperial. Sizes of base and bowl are different from Imperial sizes.

Small milk glass compote with hanging baskets and leaves on the sides – not Imperial!

Open edge carnival bowl by Fenton.

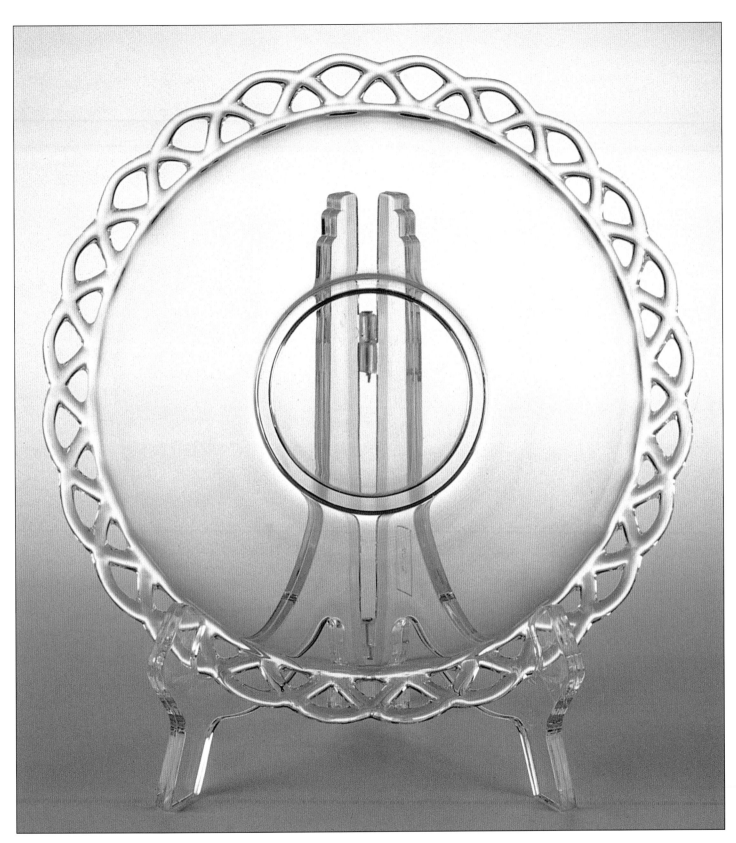

7 1/2" crystal plate with no panels, but loops are smaller than Lace Edge. A small bowl has the same loops. Neither piece is Imperial.

Some Imperial records have been lost over time. These records might have provided substantiation that the next odd piece the collector finds is Imperial. One will never know. Records were not kept of the "lunchbox pieces" made over lunch break as experiments and taken home as oddities or whimsies. Extant company records also do not document the trial periods for new pieces made for half a day but never placed into full production. With dozens of glass companies in operation workers sometimes took ideas from one job to the next and produced very similar pieces at more than one company. The last two pictures are pieces of unconfirmed origin. They may or may not be Imperial's Lace Edge. The woven pattern is Fenton's; the 4-toed shape is Imperial's; and the curve of the lace is by an unknown manufacturer.

Light blue 4-toed vase with opalescent edge and turned-in top similar to Imperial's N edge. Woven pattern is same as Fenton bowl.

Crystal 4-toed vase with opalescent edge and crimped top similar to Imperial's C edge, although Imperial did not make other vases in C. Woven pattern is same as Fenton bowl.

Chapter 9

Price List

Below is a list of Lace Edge pieces shown in Chapter 5 Mould Number List and Pictures and their approximate prices. Cut and Intaglio pieces are not listed if the plain Crystal version is known to exist. Prices for other Cut and Intaglio pieces are only slightly higher than the plain pieces for which the prices are given. A few sets are listed; for other sets, just add up the prices for the component pieces, since the pieces were also sold separately.

Prices can vary considerably by color, as noted in Chapter 4 Glass Colors. Some colors can command prices two or three or even more times the prices for Crystal. The prices below are for the least expensive color in each piece. However, for the crow's foot 749 pieces, the prices for Seafoam Blue are given, because most of the crystal pieces can be found for less than $5.

Bargains can be found at flea markets. On-line auction prices vary greatly, depending on the required opening bid and whether bidders decide to keep bidding higher and higher. The prices listed here are based on hours of hunting through glass shows and antique malls all around the country. The author takes no responsibility for reporting these prices.

11/743K	5" Vase	$22-25		1950/271	5" Heart	$18-20
11/743N	5 1/2" Vase	$22-25		1950/272	6" Heart	$18-20
11/743B	5 1/4" Vase	$22-25		1950/273	7" Heart	$18-20
11/743X	4 1/2" Vase	$22-25		1950/274C	7" Compote	$28-31
11/7455B	6 1/2" Nappy	$18-20		1950/274K	5 1/2" Compote	$28-31
11/7455D	7 1/2" Plate	$14-16		1950/275D	12" Plate	$22-25
11/7455F	6 3/4" Nappy	$18-20		1950/275F	10" Bowl	$22-25
11/7455G	6" Basket Bowl	$18-20		1950/279	Twin Candleholder (pair)	$14-16
11/7803N	5" Vase	$35-40		1950/286B	5" Vase	$22-25
11/7806D	9 1/2" Plate	$18-20		1950/715	Pie Server	No data
11/7808D	12" Plate	$22-25		1950/745C	6" Bowl	$14-16
11/7808F	11" Shallow Bowl	$22-25		1950/745F	6" Bowl	$14-16
1950/30	Sugar and Cream Set	$18-20		1950/749B	7" Comport	$14-16
1950/207C	7 1/2" Bowl	$28-31		1950/749F	7" Comporte	$14-16
1950/B207C	7 1/2" Bowl, brass base	$35-40		1950/749F	7" Comporte/Brass Handle Server	$28-31
1950/207F	8" Bowl	$22-25		1950/78	9 1/2" Footed Jar	$35-40
1950/207K	5" Flower Arranger	$14-16		1950/78C	6" Candleholder (pair)	$22-25
1950/215	Partitioned Relish Tray	No data		1950/790	Sugar and Cream Set	$18-20
1950/220C	10" Footed Crimped Bowl	$35-40		1950/B790	Sugar and Cream Set, brass base	$18-20
1950/220D	12" Footed Cake Stand	$28-31		1950/1723	7 3/4" Basket	$22-25
1950/220E	12" Footed Banana Stand	$50-55		1950/1725	12 1/2" or 13" Basket	$40-45
1950/220F	10" Footed Fruit Bowl	$28-31		30	Sugar & Cream Set (Caramel Slag)	$70-75
1950/220X	9 1/2" Footed Bowl	$35-40		207B	7 3/4" Bowl	$35-38

Code	Item	Price
207C	7 1/2" Bowl	No data
207F	8" Bowl	No data
207K	5" Flower Arranger	$28-31
220D	12" Footed Cake Stand	$70-75
274C	7" 4-Toed Compote (Purple Slag)	$50-55
274C	7" 4-Toed Compote (other color)	35-40
286B	5" Vase	$28-31
701	Fork and Spoon for Salad Set	$18-20
743B	5 1/2" Vase	$28-31
743K	5" Vase	$28-31
743N	5 1/2" Vase	$28-31
743X	4 1/2" Vase	$28-31
7430B	5 1/2" Vase	$28-31
7432B	7 3/4" Bowl	$28-31
7432D	9 1/2" Plate	$18-20
7432F	8" Nappy	$22-25
7432/86	Tid Bit Set	$50-55
7435	7" Bowl and Top	$28-31
7435C	7" Compote	$28-31
7436/5B	7 3/4" Bowl	$22-25
7436	7" Bowl and Top	$22-25
7436C	7 1/2" Bowl	$22-25
7436D	9 1/2" Plate	$18-20
7436F	8" Bowl	$18-20
7436K	5" Flower Arranger	$18-20
7436/5V	8 1/2" Plate	$28-31
7436/5X	8" Bowl	$28-31
745	Ivy Ball with Chain	$14-16
745	Ivy Ball (Upright)	$28-31
745C	6" Bowl	$14-16
745E	7" Basket Bowl	$28-31
745F	6" Bowl	$18-20
7455B	6 1/2" Nappy	18-20
7455D	7 1/2" Plate	$14-16
7455F	6 3/4" Nappy	$18-20
7455G	5" Basket Bowl	$18-20
749	4 1/2" Candleholder (pair) (Crystal)	$18-20
749	4 1/2" Candleholder (pair) (Seafoam Blue)	$170-180
749	Sugar and Creamer Set	$70-75
749	Cup and Saucer	$60-65
749	13" Oval Platter	$170-180
749	9 ounce Tumbler	$50-55
749B	7" Comporte	$28-31
749C	7" Compote	$28-31
749C	3-pc Mayonnaise Set	$150-160
749/1	11" Oval Vegetable Bowl	$160-170
749/2	11" Oval Divided Vegetable Bowl	$170-180
7494X	4 1/2" Fruit	$28-31
7495D	6 1/2" Bread and Butter Plate	$22-25
7495W	5 1/2" Cereal Bowl	$35-40
7496D	8" Salad Plate	$35-40
7496W	7" Soup Bowl	$40-45
7497B	9" Bowl	$28-31
7497/3C	8 1/2" Bowl	$28-31
7497D	11" Plate	$18-20
7497E	9 1/2" Basket Bowl	$28-31
7497F	9 1/2" Bowl	$18-20
7497K	6 1/2" Rose Bowl and Holder	$28-31
7497N	6 1/2" Flower Bowl	$28-31
7497R	6 1/2" Flower Bowl and Holder	$28-31
7497/9	Tid Bit Set	$70-75
7498B	10" Bowl	$35-40
7498/4C	10" Bowl	$35-40
7498D	12" Plate	$22-25
7498D	Cheese & Cracker Set	No data
7498F	11" Bowl	$18-20
7498K	7 1/2" Rose Bowl and Holder	$35-40
7498N	7 1/2" Flower Bowl	$35-40
7498R	7 1/2" Flower Bowl and Holder	$35-40
7498/97	Tid Bit Set	$70-75
7499B	12" Orange Bowl	$50-55
7499D	14" Plate	$22-25
7499F	13" Fruit Bowl	$35-40
7499N	8 1/2" Flower Bowl	$40-45
7499V	13" Torte Plate	No data
7499/4V	13" Cabaret Plate	No data
74910D	10" Dinner Plate	$150-160
74910X	9" Round Vegetable	$170-180
74910/6	Tid Bit Set	$190-200
78	Footed Bowl & Cover (Caramel Slag)	$115-125
78	Footed Bowl & Cover (other colors)	$28-31

Code	Item	Price	Code	Item	Price
78C	Candleholder Crimped (pair)	$28-31	7802/0	7 3/4" Basket	$50-55
78C/754	2-pc Epergne	$140-150	7803B	5" Vase	$22-25
78K	Candleholder (pair)	$28-31	7803K	5" Vase	$22-25
780	Coaster	$40-45	7803N	5" Vase	$22-25
Irice	Clock	$85-90	7804B	5 1/2" Ftd. Jelly	$18-20
780	4 1/2" Candleholder (pair)	$18-20	7804F	6 1/2" Ftd. Jelly	$18-20
780	6" Covered Bowl (Purple Slag)	$60-65	7805B	5 1/2" Low Comporte	$18-20
780	6" Covered Bowl (other color)	$35-40	7805D	7 1/2" Plate	$14-16
780	Oyster Cocktail	$40-45	7805D	8" Plate	$14-16
780	5 1/2 oz. Ftd. Juice Tumbler	$40-45	7805F	6 1/2" Nappy	$14-16
780	3 1/2 oz. Cocktail	$40-45	7805K	3" Sweet Pea	$14-16
780	4 1/2 oz. Claret Wine	$40-45	7805S	6" Square Nappy	$14-16
780	12 oz. Ftd. Ice Tea	$60-65	7805W	5 1/2" Deep Bowl	$14-16
780	10 oz. Goblet	$60-65	7806B	7 3/4" Bowl	$22-25
780	5 1/2 oz. Tall Sherbet	$40-45	7806C	7 3/4" Bowl	$22-25
780	Low Compote	$22-25	7806D	9 1/2" Plate	$10-20
780	Sugar & Creamer Set - old style	$40-45	7806/3E	8 1/2" Basket Bowl	$35-40
780	Sugar & Creamer Set - new style	$35-40	7806F	8" Walnut Bowl	$18-20
780	14-pc Punch Set (Purple Slag)	$2000-2500	7806K	4 1/2" Flower Bowl	$22-25
780C	2-pc. Epergne	$170-180	7806N	5 1/2" Flower Bowl	$22-25
780D	12 1/2" Ftd. Cake Stand	$40-45	7806/3X	8" Bowl	$28-31
780F	10" Ftd. Fruit Stand	$35-40	7806/0	9 1/2" Basket	$70-75
7800	3-pc Mayonnaise Set	$35-40	7808B	8" Trumpet Bouquet	$60-65
7800	11 1/2" Relish Dish	$22-25	7808B	10" Bowl	$22-25
7801	10 1/2" Hors d'oeuvres	$22-25	7808C	10" Bowl	$22-25
7801C	7 1/2" Compote	$28-31	7808D	12" Plate	$22-25
7801F	7 1/2" Compote	$28-31	7808F	11" Bowl (Crystal)	$28-31
7801K	5" Vase	$28-31	7808F	11" Bowl (Purple Slag)	$235-245
7801S	6" Square Bon Bon	$28-31	7808K	7" Narcissus bowl	$40-45
7801W	7 1/2" Comport	$28-31	7808K	8" Bud Bouquet	$60-65
7801Z	4 1/2" Rose Bowl	$28-31	7808N	7" Flower Bowl	$40-45
7802	10" Celery Dish	$40-45	7808/0	12 1/2" Basket	$140-150
7802B	6" Bowl	$14-16	7809B	10 1/2 Salad Bowl	$28-31
7802D	7 1/2" Plate	$14-16	7809C	12" Bowl	$35-40
7802F	6 1/2" Nappy	$14-16	7809D	14" Plate	$28-31
7802K	3 1/2" Flower Bowl	$14-16	78010	14-pc Punch Bowl Set	$115-125
7802N	5" Flower Bowl	$18-20	78010D	17" Plate	$70-75

Bibliography

Archer, Margaret and Douglas. *Imperial Glass*. Paducah, Kentucky: Collectors Books, 1998.

Co-Operative Flint Glass Co., Beaver Falls, Pa (soft-bound collection of sketches). Pittsburgh, Pennsylvania: Robt. Rawsthorne Engraving Co., lithographer. N.p., n.d.

Garrison, Myrna and Bob. *Imperial's Boudoir, Etcetera...A Comprehensive Look at Dresser Accessories for Irice and Others*. Marceline, Missouri: Walsworth Publishing Company, 1996.

——. *Milk Glass: Imperial Glass Corporation Plus Opaque, Slag, and More*. Atglen, Pennsylvania: Schiffer Publishing Ltd., 2001.

Imperial Catalogs, Photographs, Price Lists, and Salesmen's Notebooks. 1936-1977.

Measell, James, and Berry Wiggins. *Great American Glass of The Roaring 20s & Depression Era. Books 1 and 2*. Marietta, Ohio: The Glass Press, Inc., dba Antique Publications, 1998-2000.

National Imperial Glass Collectors Society. *Imperial Glass Encyclopedia*. 3 vols. Ed. by James Measell. Marietta, Ohio: The Glass Press, Inc., dba Antique Publications, 1995-1999.

Over, Naomi L. *Ruby Glass of the 20th Century*. Ed. by Tom Klopp. Marietta, Ohio: Antique Publications, 1990.

Weatherman, Hazel Marie. *Colored Glassware of the Depression Era. Book 2*. Ozark, Missouri: Weatherman Glassbooks, 1974.